Collins

阿加莎·克里斯蒂经典侦探作品集

Agatha Christie

地 狱 之 旅
Destination Unknown

〔英〕阿加莎·克里斯蒂 著

商务印书馆
2019年·北京

Agatha Christie

Destination Unknown

ⓒHarperCollins Publishers Ltd. (2012)

ⓒEnglish-Chinese simplified character rights

The Commercial Press (2019)

出 版 说 明

商务印书馆创立以来，始终以"昌明教育，开启民智"为己任，致力于移译西学、沟通中外，坚持以高质量的出版物促进文化交流，以传播先进思想推动社会进步。近年来更是加大了外语学习读物的出版，如推出了"莎翁戏剧经典"丛书等。此次引进"阿加莎·克里斯蒂经典侦探作品集"系列，是我馆开发英语学习读物的又一成果。

阿加莎·克里斯蒂（Agatha Christie 1890—1976）是英国著名女侦探小说家、剧作家，三大推理文学宗师之一，被誉为举世公认的推理小说女王。其作品已被翻译成一百多种语言，曾多次被搬上银幕。代表作有《东方快车谋杀案》和《尼罗河上的惨案》等，在中国有大批爱好者，读者接受度很高。

这套"阿加莎·克里斯蒂经典侦探作品集"丛书，是英国柯林斯出版公司精选的阿加莎·克里斯蒂的经典作品，由英国语言和文学专家专门为世界各地母语非英语的读者改编设计，每篇小说经过适当删减，其中的词汇和语法也做了简化，是适合中等以上英语水平读者学习的英语读物。

为方便读者使用，中文注释本以脚注的形式给难词标注词性和释义；提供英汉对照的作者简介、出场人物表及文化注释；书中以二维码和点读形式提供的原文朗读音频由英国本土人士录制，声情并茂地再现精彩的故事内容。

希望这套"阿加莎·克里斯蒂经典侦探作品集"丛书，能够帮助读者在欣赏英文小说的同时学习英语、提高英语能力，成为读者英语阅读和学习的最佳选择。

商务印书馆编辑部

2019 年 5 月

目　录

作者简介 ……………………………………… 4
人物表 ………………………………………… 6
正文 …………………………………………… 1
文化注释 ……………………………………… 117

作者简介

Agatha Christie (1890-1976) is known throughout the world as the Queen of Crime. Her books have sold over a billion copies in English with another billion in over 100 foreign languages. She is the most widely published and translated author of all time and in any language; only the Bible and Shakespeare have sold more copies. She is the author of 80 crime novels and short story collections, 19 plays, and six other novels. *The Mousetrap*, her most famous play, was first staged in 1952 in London and is still performed there — it is the longest-running play in history.

Agatha Christie's first novel was published in 1920. It featured Hercule Poirot, the Belgian detective who has become the most popular detective in crime fiction since Sherlock Holmes. Collins has published Agatha Christie since 1926.

阿加莎·克里斯蒂

阿加莎·克里斯蒂(1890—1976)在世界各地被誉为"侦探小说女王"。她以英语出版的作品销量超过十亿册,而以一百多种外语出版的作品销量也达到了十亿册。她是迄今为止以各语种得到最广泛出版和译介的作家,其作品销量仅次于《圣经》和莎士比亚的作品。她著有80部侦探题材的长篇小说和短篇小说集、19部剧作及其他6部小说。《捕鼠器》是她最有名的剧作,1952年在伦敦被首次搬上舞台,直到今天还在上演——它也成为历史上演出时间最长的戏剧。

阿加莎·克里斯蒂的第一部小说出版于1920年,其中塑造了比利时大侦探赫尔克里·波洛这一人物——他已成为自夏洛克·福尔摩斯以来犯罪小说里最知名的侦探。柯林斯出版公司自1926年至今一直在出版阿加莎·克里斯蒂的作品。

人物表

Mr Jessop：为英国情报部门工作

Colonel Wharton：为英国情报部门工作

Thomas（Tom）Betterton：著名英国科学家，发现了 ZE 裂变。起初与 Elsa 结婚，后又与 Olive 结婚

Dr Mannheim：Thomas Betterton 的第一任妻子 Elsa 的父亲，Boris Glydr 的叔叔

Olive Betterton：科学家 Thomas Betterton 的新任（第二任）妻子

Walter Griffiths：Thomas Betterton 的美国朋友

Carol Speeder：Thomas Betterton 的美国朋友

Major Boris Glydr：来自波兰，Thomas Betterton 第一任妻子 Elsa 的堂弟

Hilary Craven：在摩洛哥卡萨布兰卡旅行的女子（她的女儿 Brenda 刚刚去世，她的丈夫 Nigel 抛弃了她）

Mrs Baker：在摩洛哥旅行的美国中年女子

Miss Hetherington：在摩洛哥旅行的英国中年女子

Henri Laurier：在摩洛哥工作的法国男子

Mr Aristides：希腊老人，世界上最富有的人之一

Andrew（Andy）Peters：美国科学家

Torquil Ericsson：挪威科学家

Dr Barron：法国科学家

Helga Needheim：德国科学家

Dr Van Heidem："单位"（the Unit）的副主管

Dr Rubec：在"单位"工作的瑞士医生

Miss Jenson：在"单位"为主管工作的女子

Mademoiselle La Roche：在"单位"负责服装部门

Dr Simon Murchison：与 Tom Betterton 共事的科学家，是 Bianca 的丈夫

Bianca Murchison：Simon Murchison 的意大利妻子

Monsieur Leblanc：为法国情报部门工作，是 Jessop 的同事

The Director：掌管"单位"的男子

Mohammed：在"单位"工作的摩洛哥男子

French Minister：法国政府内的要人

American Ambassador：在摩洛哥代表美国的要人

Journalist：为著名报纸撰稿的男子

Lord Alverstoke：退休的英国最高法官

Agatha Christie

Destination Unknown

Chapter 1

Mr Jessop sat at his desk. He was a man who looked as if he lived indoors① — a man of desks and paper — and his office was at the end of a long underground corridor. Although Jessop's smooth, pale face had no expression, his eyes were tired.

Walking with nervous energy up and down Jessop's office was Colonel② Wharton. The Colonel had dark hair and a small moustache. 'Reports!' he exclaimed loudly, 'All we get is security reports and they're all useless!'

Jessop looked down at the papers and documents on his desk. They all read, '*Betterton, Thomas*'.

'Reports — not just from Rome,' continued the Colonel, 'but from nearly every capital city in the world!' He sat down abruptly③. 'We've got to find Thomas Betterton,' he insisted. 'He's like all these other top scientists that have disappeared recently — we still don't know where they are. And we don't know how or why they disappear, either,' he added. 'Have you read the latest information on Betterton from America?'

Jessop nodded. 'Betterton worked in America before the war,' he said. 'His work was good, but ordinary. When the scientist Dr Mannheim escaped to America from Germany, Betterton worked as his assistant, and he later married Dr Mannheim's daughter, Elsa. After Dr Mannheim died, Betterton worked on his own, and became very famous when he discovered ZE Fission④ — one of the most brilliant and important

---

① indoors *adv.* 在室内 ② colonel *n.* 上校 ③ abruptly *adv.* 莽撞地
④ fission *n.* 裂变

discoveries about nuclear science[①] that's ever been made.'

'I don't understand ZE Fission at all,' said Colonel Wharton, 'or anything about atom bombs or nuclear science. All I know is that these scientists now have the power to destroy the world!'

'Betterton became one of the most important scientists in the world,' continued Jessop. 'But his wife Elsa died soon after their marriage and Betterton decided to come to England. He's been working at the nuclear laboratory[②] in Harwell for the last eighteen months. Just six months ago he married again.'

'What about Betterton's second wife?' asked Wharton. 'Anything of interest?'

Jessop shook his head. 'We can't find anything,' he said. 'She's the daughter of a local lawyer and worked in an office before her marriage.'

'What do the people at Harwell say about Betterton?' Wharton asked.

'They said that he was a pleasant man,' Jessop replied. 'He worked on the practical uses of ZE Fission — nothing new or original.'

Both men were silent for a moment, as they looked at the big pile of security reports on the desk. 'Was Betterton thoroughly investigated before he arrived in England?' asked Colonel Wharton.

'Yes, of course. Everything was satisfactory.'

'And Betterton's been here eighteen months,' said Wharton thoughtfully. 'Sometimes these scientists get nervous and upset because they're always watched so carefully — for security reasons, of course. They begin to dream of an ideal world — peace

---

① nuclear science *n.* 核科学　② laboratory *n.* 实验室

and freedom for everyone. They want to share their secrets and their work with all the world, for the good of humanity①! That's exactly the moment when someone can persuade them to sell their secrets and betray② their country.'

'It would help if I knew more about Betterton,' said Jessop, looking again at the papers on his desk. 'Not about his work, but about the everyday things — what made him laugh, the people he admired or what made him angry.'

'Can't his wife tell you that?' asked Wharton.

'She hasn't helped me much so far,' said Jessop. 'She says she doesn't know anything about her husband's disappearance — she says she thinks he's been kidnapped③.'

'What's she like?'

'She seems like a very ordinary woman,' said Jessop. 'She's waiting to see me now. I'll ask her the same questions again and see if she can tell me anything new.'

Wharton nodded. 'It's the only way,' he said. 'Let me know if you learn anything interesting.' He left the room as Jessop picked up the phone and told his assistant to send in Mrs Betterton.

Mrs Olive Betterton was a tall woman of about twenty-seven. The first thing you noticed about her was her beautiful red hair. Because her hair was so lovely, you didn't really notice what her face looked like. She had blue-green eyes and light eyelashes④.

'Oh, Mr Jessop,' she said breathlessly⑤ as she sat down, 'is there any news?'

'No, I'm sorry,' said Jessop gently. 'There's no definite

---

① humanity *n*. 人类　② betray *v*. 背叛　③ kidnap *v*. 绑架　④ eyelash *n*. 睫毛　⑤ breathlessly *adv*. 上气不接下气地

news. I just wanted to ask you the same questions in case you remember some small detail that could help.'

'Yes. Yes, I understand,' said Mrs Betterton. 'I don't mind. It's better than sitting at home — wondering. Ask me any questions you like.'

'So the last time you saw your husband was on 23rd August, when he left to go to a conference in Paris?'

'Yes.'

'He went to the first two days of the conference,' said Jessop, 'but on the third day he told a colleague that he was going on a boat trip on the river Seine. Does that seem likely?'

'It is a little strange that he missed the conference,' admitted Mrs Betterton.

'He didn't return to his hotel that evening,' continued Jessop, 'and he didn't travel to another country using his own passport. Do you know if he had a second passport — in another name, perhaps?'

'No, no, of course not. And he wouldn't just go away without telling me.'

'Was his health all right?' asked Jessop.

'Yes. He was working hard and sometimes felt tired, that's all,' said Mrs Betterton. 'He wasn't worried or unhappy about anything, if that's what you mean. Something must have happened to him.' She opened her handbag and took out a handkerchief①. 'It's all so awful,' she said, her voice shaking. 'Something's happened to Tom. He's been kidnapped or — or he's dead.'

'Now please, Mrs Betterton — there's no need to think that your husband is dead. We would have found his body by now.'

---

① handkerchief *n.* 手帕

She took the handkerchief away from her eyes and stared at him, suddenly angry. 'I know what you think,' she said, 'but it's not true! Tom would never sell secrets or betray his country. He was a scientist — a brilliant scientist.'

'Yes,' agreed Jessop, 'he was a brilliant scientist. That's why he might have been offered a large amount of money to work in another country.'

'It's not true,' repeated Olive Betterton angrily. 'He would have told me. He would have given me some clue. But he told me nothing. I don't know where he is. He must have been kidnapped — or he's dead. But I need to know, I must know. I can't go on like this, waiting and wondering. I can't eat or sleep. I'm sick with worry. Can't you help me? Can't you help me at all?'

'I'm very sorry, Mrs Betterton,' said Jessop gently. 'We're doing our best to find out what's happened to your husband. We get lots of reports every day, but there is still no definite news.'

'I must *know*,' she said again. 'I can't go on like this.'

'Do you love your husband, Mrs Betterton?'

'Of course I love him. We've only been married six months.'

'So you hadn't argued with him before he disappeared?'

'Oh, no!'

'And there was — I'm sorry to ask — no other woman?'

'Of course not. I've told you. We were only married in April.'

'I'm sorry, but we have to think of everything,' said Jessop. 'I'm trying to find out what your husband was like. And you're not helping me very much.'

'But I've answered all your questions.'

'Yes, you have,' said Jessop, 'but your answers are mainly negative — I want something *positive*, something that tells me the kind of person your husband is.'

She thought for a moment. 'Well,' she said, 'Tom was cheerful and good-tempered①. And clever, of course.'

Jessop sighed. 'Did your husband have many friends?'

'He was in America for so long,' said Mrs Betterton, 'that he didn't know many people here.'

Jessop looked at a paper on his desk. 'I have a report here,' he said, 'that two people from America visited your husband recently. The first was called Walter Griffiths.'

'Yes, I remember him. Tom was surprised to see him, but very pleased. They were good friends in America. Griffiths was very anxious to tell Tom everything that had happened after he left — all the local gossip②, I suppose. I didn't listen very closely.'

'And the second person to visit your husband was a woman called Carol Speeder.'

'Oh, yes. She had known Tom in America, and rang him up from London to ask if we could meet for lunch. But we didn't go in the end.'

'You didn't go, but your husband did.'

'What?' Mrs Betterton stared at him.

'So he didn't tell you? It was on 12th August.'

Mrs Betterton looked uneasy. 'Yes, Tom did go to London then.'

'Did you notice any change in your husband's behaviour about that time? It was a week before the conference.'

'No — no, I noticed nothing,' she said. 'There was nothing

---

① good-tempered *adj.* 好脾气的 ② gossip *n.* 闲话

to notice.'

The telephone on Jessop's desk rang and he picked up the receiver.

'There's a man asking to see you, Sir,' said his assistant. 'About Thomas Betterton.' He spelt out a foreign name that Jessop wrote down on a piece of paper.

'Is he from Poland?' Jessop asked.

'He didn't say, Sir. He speaks English well.'

'Ask him to wait,' Jessop said. 'I'll see him in a minute.' He put down the phone.

'Do you know anybody with this name?' Jessop asked, showing Mrs Betterton the paper.

Her eyes widened and he thought she looked frightened.

'Yes,' she said. 'Yes, I do. He wrote to me yesterday. He's a cousin of Tom's first wife. He has just arrived in England and wrote to say how sorry he was that Tom had disappeared. He asked if I had any news.'

'Did your husband ever talk about him?'

'No.'

'So he might not be any relation at all?'

'Well, no, I suppose not. I didn't think of that.' Olive Betterton looked surprised. 'But Tom's first wife was Dr Mannheim's daughter. This man knew all about her. And why else would he write to me?'

'I don't know,' admitted Jessop. 'I'm afraid in this job I'm always a little suspicious[①] of everyone.'

'Yes, I can understand that,' said Mrs Betterton. She pushed her red hair back from her forehead. 'I can't bear it much longer,' she said nervously. 'Just sitting and waiting. I want to

---

① suspicious *adj.* 感觉可疑的

get away — go abroad for a while. Somewhere where the newspaper reporters won't ring me up all the time, and people won't stare at me. I've tried to be brave, but it's too much for me. My doctor agrees. He wrote me a letter.'

She took an envelope out of her bag and gave it to Jessop. 'See what my doctor says.'

Jessop read the letter. 'Yes,' he said. 'Yes, I see.' He gave the letter back.

'So — can I go?' she asked nervously.

'Oh, of course, Mrs Betterton,' Jessop replied in surprise. 'Why not? It's entirely your own business. Just let me know how I can contact you in case there's news. Where are you going?'

'Somewhere sunny — Spain or Morocco.'

'Very nice,' said Jessop. 'I'm sure it will be good for you.'

'Oh, yes, thank you. Thank you very much.' Mrs Betterton stood up, excited and nervous, and Jessop showed her out of the room.

When she had gone, Jessop sat down at his desk. Then he smiled, very slowly.

He picked up the phone. 'I'll see Major Glydr now,' he said.

Chapter 2

'Major Glydr?' Jessop hesitated as he said the strange name.

'It is difficult to say, yes,' said the visitor. 'Now I live in America, I think I will change my name.'

'Have you just arrived from America?'

'Yes, I arrived a week ago.'

Jessop looked at his visitor. He saw a tall man, who stood very straight and stiff①, aged about thirty. His fair hair was cut very short, and he spoke slowly and carefully. He seemed to be in complete control of himself, and wasn't at all nervous.

'How can I help you?' Jessop asked.

'I came to ask if you had any news about Thomas Betterton. He is a relative of mine by marriage②.'

'I'm sorry, but I have no definite news,' said Jessop pleasantly. 'I am told, Major Glydr, that you are the nephew of the late Dr Mannheim.'

'Ah, so you know that already. Yes, my mother was Dr Mannheim's only sister. I am from Poland, but my parents died when I was young and I went to live in Germany with my uncle and his daughter, Elsa. She was like a sister to me. Then came World War II, and my uncle and Elsa escaped to America while I stayed to fight in the Polish Resistance③ against the Germans.

'After the war I finally get to America, but alas' — he spread out his hands — 'my uncle, he is dead, my cousin, too, and

---

① stiff *adj*. 僵硬的;不友好的 ② by marriage 与婚姻有关的 ③ resistance *n*. 秘密抵抗组织

her husband has come to England and has married again. So once more I have no family. When I hear about the disappearance of the well-known scientist Thomas Betterton, I come over to see what can be done.' He paused and looked at Jessop. 'Do you know why he disappeared?'

Jessop's face had no expression. 'We do not,' he replied.

'But you suspect?'

'It is possible,' said Jessop carefully, 'that his disappearance is connected to that of other scientists.'

'Did all these scientists disappear willingly①?'

'It is difficult to say,' said Jessop. 'Forgive me for asking, Major Glydr, but Thomas Betterton is related to you only by marriage. You don't know him. Why are you so interested?'

'That is true. But in Poland the family is very important.' He stood up and bowed②. 'I thank you for your time.'

'I'm sorry I cannot help you,' said Jessop. 'But if I do have any news, where can I contact you?'

'The American Embassy will know how to find me. I thank you.' Again Major Glydr bowed and then left the room.

Back at his desk, Jessop picked up the phone. 'Ask Colonel Wharton to come to my office.'

When Wharton entered the room Jessop said, 'Something is happening at last. Mrs Betterton wants to go abroad.'

'Is she going to meet her husband?'

'I hope so,' said Jessop. 'She showed me a letter from her doctor, advising a rest and a change of scene③. Of course, it may even be true.'

'Do you really think so?'

---

① willingly *adv.* 愿意地　② bow *v.* 鞠躬　③ change of scene 换个环境

'No, I don't. But she's very good at pretending — very convincing①.'

'Did you find out anything else?' asked Wharton.

'Just that Betterton didn't tell his wife that he met Carol Speeder for lunch,' said Jessop. 'She might be the contact. And she had a letter from Major Glydr, a cousin of Betterton's first wife. He's just been here himself. We'll keep a close eye on him.'

'Where is Mrs Betterton going?'

'Spain or Morocco, she said.'

'They are the only two countries where Betterton *hasn't* been seen,' said Wharton. 'All right, we'll watch her very carefully. We'll use Janet, I think. Let's hope we get results this time.'

Jessop leaned back in his chair. 'It's a long time since I had a holiday,' he said. 'I might even take a trip abroad myself...'

---

① convincing *adj.* 有说服力的

Chapter 3

I

'Air France Flight 108 to Paris is now boarding.'

On hearing this announcement, Hilary Craven and the rest of the passengers walked out to the waiting aeroplane at Heathrow Airport. 'This is it,' thought Hilary as she took her seat on the plane. 'I'm finally going to escape. Away from the cold and grey, the pain and misery①, to sunshine, blue skies and a new life.'

The plane moved gently along the runway②, and the air hostess told the passengers to fasten their seat belts. With a roar of the engines the plane took off, and soon they were flying up in the clouds. The roads and railways, so far below, looked small and unimportant. Hilary closed her eyes. She had escaped. She had left England, left Nigel, and left Brenda's grave③ behind her. She sat back in her seat and went to sleep.

II

When Hilary woke up, the plane was landing — but not in Paris.

'We are landing at Beauvais because of thick fog in Paris,' explained the air hostess. Once they were on the ground, the passengers walked through the cold damp mist to a rough

---

① misery *n*. 痛苦　② runway *n*. 跑道　③ grave *n*. 坟墓

wooden building. 'It's an old war aerodrome①,' Hilary heard a man say. 'At least we're in France, so we should get something to drink.'

True enough, the passengers were soon given drinks while they waited. Hours passed and other planes landed. Soon the small building was full of cold, tired people, complaining about the delay.

Hilary felt like she was in a dream. She waited patiently until she was finally seated on a bus, which began its long slow journey through the fog towards Paris. It was midnight when the passengers at last arrived at their hotel, and Hilary was so tired that she went straight to bed.

Her plane to Casablanca in Morocco was due to leave Paris at ten-thirty the next morning, but when Hilary arrived at the airport everything was in confusion. Because of the fog, planes had been delayed all over Europe. After a long wait, Hilary was finally booked onto another flight to Casablanca.

'The fog has caused many delays,' explained the busy clerk at the departure desk. 'But this plane will arrive in Casablanca only three hours later than your original flight. And what does it really matter, Madame, which plane you take to Casablanca?'

But on that day it did matter. When Hilary finally arrived at Casablanca and stepped out into the sunshine, the porter in charge of the luggage trolley said, 'It was lucky for you, Madame, that you were not on the earlier plane.'

'Why?' Hilary asked. 'What happened?'

The man looked around uneasily②, but he knew that the news could not be kept secret. 'It was terrible,' he said quietly.

---

① aerodrome *n.* 小型飞机场 ② uneasily *adv.* 不安地

'The plane crashed. Only a few people are still alive. They have been taken to hospital, badly hurt.'

Hilary's first reaction was anger. 'If I had been on that plane,' she thought, 'I would be dead now — it would all be over, at last…'

She went through customs and was driven to her hotel. She had arrived. She had left cold, dark London behind and now she was in a place of life and colour and sunshine. It was just as lovely as she had imagined it would be. She had escaped.

But finally, sitting in her hotel room, Hilary realized that there *was* no escape. Brenda was still dead, and soon Nigel would be marrying his new wife. Those were the facts and they wouldn't change. She still felt the same despair①, whatever country she was in. There was no escape from reality.

Hilary had survived② a long illness, and then her husband Nigel had cruelly abandoned③ her. She had survived because she had Brenda, her daughter. But then Brenda had become ill, and finally she had died …

Thinking with despair about her husband and her daughter, Hilary finally admitted that she did not want to live any more. She wished she had died in the plane crash. It would have been so easy. If she had been on her original flight, she would now be dead, and free from suffering④. 'Well,' thought Hilary at last, 'I can still end it now. I just need to go to a pharmacy.'

III

Hilary was surprised to find that sleeping pills⑤ were hard to

---

① despair *n.* 绝望　② survive *v.* 幸存　③ abandon *v.* 抛弃　④ suffering *n.* 痛苦　⑤ sleeping pill *n.* 安眠药

buy in a foreign city. The first pharmacy did not give her enough, saying that for more pills she needed a prescription①. On her way out she bumped into② a tall, serious young man who said 'Sorry' in English. She heard him ask for a particular kind of toothpaste as she left the shop.

She visited four different pharmacies before she had enough sleeping pills. In the third pharmacy, Hilary was amused to see the serious young man again, still asking for toothpaste. And when she went downstairs for dinner, Hilary noticed the young man in the hotel dining room, reading a French newspaper.

After a good meal and a glass of wine, Hilary felt almost excited about what she was going to do. It was her last adventure. She went back to her room carrying a bottle of water, locked the door and took out all the sleeping pills. She just had to swallow the pills and her life would be over.

Though she was a little afraid, Hilary was also calm. She decided not to leave a note — Nigel would read about her death in the newspaper. He didn't seem important any more. She could do what she wanted, and she was ready to start her final journey.

But as Hilary reached for the first sleeping pill she heard a quiet knock on the door. She frowned③ and decided not to answer it. But after a while there was another knock, and Hilary watched in amazement as the key slowly turned in the lock and the door opened. In came the serious young man who had been trying to buy toothpaste.

'What do you think you're doing here?' asked Hilary angrily.

'That's just what I was going to ask you,' said the serious

---

① prescription *n*. 处方 ② bump into *v*. 撞上 ③ frown *v*. 皱眉

young man, looking at the pills on the table.

The situation was so strange that Hilary didn't know what to say. In the end she asked, 'How did you turn the key in the lock?'

'Oh, that!' The young man smiled and showed her a metal instrument. 'You put it in the lock and turn the key from the outside,' he explained. 'Burglars[①] use them.'

'So you're a burglar?' said Hilary.

'No, no,' said the young man. 'My name's Jessop. I did knock, if you remember. You wouldn't let me in so I used this.'

'But why?'

Again Jessop looked at the pills on the table. 'It's not like going to sleep,' he said. 'If it works at all, it can take a long time, and can be very painful.'

Hilary forced herself to smile. 'Do you think I was going to kill myself?' she said. 'That's ridiculous!'

'I know you were,' replied Jessop. 'I followed you to those pharmacies and saw you buy all those sleeping pills.' His voice was friendly and casual.

Hilary stopped pretending 'You can't stop me,' she said. 'Even if you take the pills away, I can get some more. Or I could jump off a roof, or in front of a train.'

'No,' he agreed. 'I can't stop you, but tomorrow you might not do anything. Tomorrow you might feel differently.'

'I don't think I will,' Hilary argued. 'My husband, who I loved, left me. My only child died painfully. I don't have any close friends or relatives, and I don't have any work or a job that I love doing. I don't think it's wrong to end my own life.

---

① burglar *n.* 窃贼

So why don't you just leave me alone?'

The young man looked at her thoughtfully. 'So, let's make sure I understand. You don't want to live any longer — is that right?'

'Yes, that's right.'

'Good,' said Jessop, cheerfully. 'Instead of sleeping pills, I'm going to suggest another way that you can die.'

'I don't understand what you mean,' said Hilary in surprise.

'Let me explain,' said Jessop. 'You may have heard that several scientists have disappeared lately?'

'Yes,' said Hilary. 'I've read about it in the newspapers.'

'Well,' continued Jessop, 'we want to know what's happened to them. Were all these scientists — there are lots of them — kidnapped, or did they go willingly? Where have they gone? Who arranged everything and what do they want? There are so many questions — and you can help us get some answers.'

Hilary stared at him. 'Me? How?'

'A scientist called Thomas Betterton disappeared from Paris just over two months ago. His wife says she has no idea where he is. I don't think that's true.'

Hilary leaned forward, interested in what he said, briefly forgetting her own problems.

'We watched Mrs Betterton closely,' continued Jessop. 'Yesterday she left England to travel to Casablanca. Her plane crashed.'

'I know about the plane,' said Hilary. 'I was supposed to be on it.'

'Mrs Betterton is in hospital at the moment,' said Jessop, 'but the doctor says she won't live for long.'

'I still don't understand,' said Hilary. 'What does this have to do with me?'

'Because you have red hair, the same as Mrs Betterton,' explained Jessop. 'I'm suggesting that when Mrs Betterton dies, you take her place. You pretend to be Mrs Betterton. You try and reach her husband and find out where he is and what he's doing.'

'But surely,' said Hilary, 'they would know I wasn't really her?'

'We don't know for sure,' said Jessop. 'Often these people work in small groups for their own security. If Mrs Betterton was travelling to meet her husband, all that the people here in Morocco know is that they have to contact a certain woman at a certain time and place. Mrs Betterton's passport description is five-foot-seven, red hair, blue-green eyes — just like you.

'We will arrange things with the French authorities so that officially you — Hilary Craven — died in hospital a few days after the plane crash. Mrs Betterton will continue her journey. And being in a plane crash is a good cover story① for you. Concussion② can cause loss of memory.'

'It's a crazy idea!' Hilary exclaimed.

'Oh, yes,' said Jessop. 'It *is* crazy. It's very difficult and dangerous, and if I'm being honest, your chances of surviving aren't high — you may well be killed. But that's what you want, isn't it? And this way will probably be more exciting than sleeping pills.'

Suddenly and unexpectedly Hilary laughed. 'I do believe you're right,' she said. 'I'll do it. Yes, I'll do it.'

'In that case,' said Jessop, standing up with sudden energy, 'there's no time to lose.'

---

① cover story *n.* (掩护身份用的)托词　② concussion *n.* 脑震荡

Chapter 4

I

In the hospital Olive Betterton lay unconscious① in bed. The doctor quietly told Jessop that she wouldn't live much longer.

'What do you want me to say to her?' asked Hilary.

'Find out any information you can,' replied Jessop. 'Any password②, sign or message — anything that might help. She is more likely to speak to you than to me.'

Hilary nodded and went to sit by Olive Betterton's bed. She felt extremely sorry for the woman who lay there dying. Had she really been going to meet the man she loved?

Time passed. It wasn't until two hours later that Olive Betterton's eyes opened for a moment, and a nurse left to find the doctor. The dying woman looked at Hilary with surprise. 'Where ... ?' Mrs Betterton's voice was faint and breathless.

The doctor entered the room and held Mrs Betterton's hand. 'You are in hospital, Madame,' he said. 'There was an accident to the plane. Is there anyone you want to see in Casablanca? Any message for anyone?'

'No,' said Mrs Betterton. She looked again at Hilary. 'Who — who ... ?'

'I came from England on a plane, too,' said Hilary. 'Please tell me if I can help you.'

'No — nothing.'

---

① unconscious *adj.* 无意识的 ② password *n.* 密码

The dying woman's eyes closed again. Jessop stepped forward. 'Can you tell me anything about your husband, Mrs Betterton?'

Her eyes opened for a moment. 'No,' she said. Jessop quietly left the room. 'It won't be long,' the doctor said quietly to Hilary, before he too left the room. The two women were alone.

Olive Betterton moved her hand a little and tried to speak. It was obviously hard for her. 'Tell me — tell me...'

Hilary knew what she was asking. 'You are dying,' she said clearly. 'Please listen to me. I am going to try and reach your husband — to reach Tom. Do you have a message for him?'

'Tell him — to be careful. Boris — Boris — dangerous...' Her voice was faint.

'Is there anything you know that will help me?' asked Hilary.

'Snow,' said Olive Betterton faintly. Then she made an effort to speak. '*Snow, snow, beautiful snow! You slip on a lump*①, *and over you go!* Go — go and tell him about Boris. I didn't believe it, but perhaps it's true... If it is...' — she looked painfully up at Hilary — 'take care...'

A strange noise came from Olive Betterton's lips. And then she died.

II

Hilary worked very hard for the next five days. She stayed in a private room in the hospital and memorized all the details of Olive Betterton's life that Jessop gave her. She learned all about

---

① lump *n*. 隆起物

Olive's house, her relatives, her wedding day and her married life with Thomas Betterton. She knew all about Olive's pet dog, what she liked to eat and drink and what the rooms in her house looked like.

'Does all this really matter?' Hilary asked Jessop.

'Probably not,' he replied, 'but you've got to think that you *are* Olive Betterton. You have to *become* her in every detail. And you haven't got much time. It's a good thing that you're intelligent and have a good memory.'

He looked at her thoughtfully. Although their passport descriptions were the same, Hilary Craven and Olive Betterton looked very different. You didn't really notice Olive's face, but Hilary's face was strong, and her eyes were alive and intelligent.

Hilary was enjoying herself and was interested in what she was doing, but she still had questions. 'How do you know that the people here won't know exactly what Olive Betterton looks like?'

'I don't know for sure,' admitted Jessop. 'It is a risk. But hopefully, all they know is that Olive Betterton was arriving on that plane. She herself isn't a scientist — she's not important. It's only because of the plane crash — which was real — and your red hair, that we can take this chance. All we had planned to do before was to watch Olive Betterton — that's all.'

'Will you be watching me?' asked Hilary.

'Yes, of course,' said Jessop. 'But I won't tell you how. Then you won't be able to tell anyone else.'

'Do you think I would?'

'I don't mean on purpose,' Jessop said. 'But if someone surprises you, even a moment's pause or a look can give you away.'

The lessons continued, and Hilary learned not just about Olive Betterton, but also what she needed to do as she went on her journey. Jessop asked Hilary question after question, testing her knowledge and trying to confuse her. At last he said he was satisfied.

'You're a quick learner,' said Jessop. 'And remember, though you may feel alone at times, you probably won't be. I say "probably", but I can't promise.'

'And what happens,' said Hilary, 'if I succeed — if I finally see Tom Betterton?'

Jessop looked serious. 'Yes,' he said. 'That's the most dangerous moment. All I can say is that if everything has gone to plan, you should have protection. But at the beginning, I did say that your chances of surviving weren't high. Though that was before I knew you very well.'

Hilary was pleased. 'I have another question,' she said. 'What happens if I meet someone who recognizes me — Hilary Craven?'

'Don't worry,' said Jessop. 'The people you travelled with on the plane have flown on elsewhere. When you leave this hospital you'll be wearing Olive Betterton's clothes and your hair will be styled like hers. We have a doctor who will make it look as if you've been in an accident. No one will recognize you.'

'You think of everything,' said Hilary. 'And what do you think about what Olive Betterton told me before she died? She said "Tell him" — meaning her husband — "tell him to be careful — Boris — dangerous —"'

'Boris,' repeated Jessop. 'Yes, that's interesting. She must have meant Major Boris Glydr.'

'Do you know him?' asked Hilary. 'Who is he?'

'If he is who he says he is, he's a cousin of the first Mrs Betterton.'

'She was frightened,' said Hilary, frowning. 'Tell me what he looks like, so I can recognize him.'

'He's about six feet tall and has short fair hair, light eyes and is rather stiff.' Jessop paused. 'I had him followed when he left my office,' he said, 'but he went straight to the American Embassy. Then we lost him. But yes — I think that Olive Betterton was right when she said that Boris Glydr was dangerous.'

Chapter 5

I

Two middle-aged ladies were sitting in the small lounge of a hotel in Casablanca. Mrs Baker, short and round, with blue-tinted① hair, was writing letters. She was an energetic woman who loved to talk — a typical American travelling abroad.

Miss Hetherington, who was obviously English, was knitting② a shapeless-looking jumper. She was tall and thin with badly-styled hair and a disappointed expression.

The two ladies had been staying at the hotel for a few days and had got to know each other. They both looked up as they saw a tall woman with red hair walk past the door of the lounge.

'Did you see that woman with red hair?' whispered Mrs Baker. 'They say she's the only survivor③ of that terrible plane crash last week.'

'I saw her arrive this afternoon,' said Miss Hetherington. 'She came straight from hospital in an ambulance.'

'The hotel manager told me she had concussion,' continued Mrs Baker. 'I see her face was bandaged④. Poor thing. I wonder if she was travelling with her husband?'

'I don't think so,' said Miss Hetherington. 'In the newspaper it said she was travelling alone. Her name is Mrs

---

① tinted *adj*. 着色的　② knit *v*. 针织　③ survivor *n*. 幸存者　④ bandage *v*. 用绷带包扎

Betterton, I believe. Now where have I heard that name before?'

II

Looking pale and ill, with her face bandaged, Mrs Betterton had arrived at the hotel, where the manager showed her to her room. When he had gone, Hilary lay down on the bed, thinking that Olive Betterton would need to rest.

Olive Betterton's passport now had Hilary's photo on it and her signature was in Hilary's handwriting. Everything was organized. But there were no letters or messages for her at the hotel reception desk, and all Olive Betterton's tickets and travel plans were now out of date.

The real Olive Betterton, however, had been in a plane crash. If Hilary forgot any instructions or things she had to do next, she could blame the concussion. All she could do now was to wait and see if anything happened.

In the evening, Hilary went downstairs to the hotel dining room. People stared at her and whispered, obviously talking about the accident. After dinner Hilary sat in the lounge and picked up a magazine. She wondered if anyone would talk to her. There were one or two other women sitting in the room, and soon a small, middle-aged woman with blue-tinted hair moved to sit near her. 'Please excuse me,' the woman said in a pleasant voice with an American accent, 'but are you the woman who escaped from that plane crash?'

Hilary put down her magazine. 'Yes,' she said, 'I am.'

'That crash was terrible!' the woman said. 'Can I ask, Miss — Mrs ...'

'Betterton,' said Hilary.

'Can I ask, Mrs Betterton, if you were sitting in the front or the back of the plane?'

Hilary knew the answer to this question. 'Near the back,' she said.

'Did you hear that, Miss Hetherington?' said the woman, turning to include another middle-aged lady in the conversation. 'They do say the back of the plane is the safest place to be. I won't sit near the front again. Let me introduce myself,' the woman continued. 'My name is Mrs Baker and this is Miss Hetherington.'

Hilary politely said hello. 'I've been travelling round Morocco,' Mrs Baker continued. 'Are you planning to visit Marrakesh, Mrs Betterton?'

'Yes, I am,' said Hilary. 'But I need to rebook my tickets.'

'Marrakesh is very expensive,' said Miss Hetherington. 'Though I have heard of a nice hotel there — very clean and with good food.'

'Where else are you going, Mrs Betterton?' asked Mrs Baker.

'I would like to see Fez,' said Hilary carefully. 'Have you been there?'

'Not yet. But I'm planning to go there soon, and so is Miss Hetherington,' said Mrs Baker. 'I believe the old city is well worth seeing.'

After the three women had talked a while longer, Hilary said she was tired and went upstairs to her room. Had she achieved anything? She wasn't sure. The two women she had just talked to seemed so normal, such typical travellers. She would see if anything happened tomorrow.

The next morning there were still no letters or messages, so Hilary decided to go to the travel agency to rebook her tickets.

After waiting in the queue, she finally reached the front desk and told the clerk her name.

'Ah yes, Madame Betterton,' said the clerk. 'We received your telephone message and I have all your new tickets and travel plans ready for you.'

Hilary was excited. She hadn't phoned the travel agency. This was a definite sign that Olive Betterton's travel plans had been arranged by someone else. Outside, Hilary looked carefully at her new tickets, and saw that she was booked to leave for Fez the next day.

Back at the hotel, Hilary didn't see Mrs Baker again, and though she did see Miss Hetherington, she didn't speak to her. And the next day Hilary left by train for Fez.

Chapter 6

The weather was perfect — sunny and clear — as Hilary looked out of the train window on her way to Fez. In her carriage① was a small Frenchman who looked like a businessman, a nun② and two Moroccan ladies with lots of packages, who talked happily to each other.

The Frenchman offered to light Hilary's cigarette, and soon he was talking about Morocco and telling Hilary about some of the sights that they passed. He was an interesting and intelligent man.

'It must be a change for you,' he said, 'coming here from England — so cold, so foggy, so unpleasant.'

'Yes, it's very different here,' Hilary agreed.

'I myself travelled from Paris three weeks ago. There too there was fog and rain, while here it is all sunshine. How was the weather in England when you left?'

'Like Paris,' said Hilary. 'It was foggy.'

'Ah yes, it is the foggy season. And snow — have you had snow this year?'

'No,' said Hilary, 'there has been no snow.' She was amused that the Frenchman thought the English always talked about the weather.

The journey continued. The two Moroccan ladies got off and other travellers got on the train. It was evening when they arrived at Fez.

Hilary stood on the station platform, confused by the noise

---

① carriage *n*. 车厢 ② nun *n*. 修女

and the shouts of all the porters who wanted to take her luggage. 'Let me help you, Madame,' said the Frenchman. 'I believe you said you are staying at the Palais Jamaï? It is eight kilometres from here.'

'It's not in the town, then?' Hilary asked.

'It is by the old town,' the Frenchman explained. 'Me, I am staying here in the city, but the Palais Jamaï is where people go to relax. It has beautiful gardens, and from there you can go straight to the old city of Fez. I will arrange a taxi for you.'

'You're very kind,' said Hilary gratefully.

The Frenchman arranged everything for her, and just before she left, he gave Hilary his card, which read *Monsieur Henri Laurier*.

Hilary sat nervously in the taxi. Was she really going to her hotel or was this where her journey into the unknown began? But soon she did indeed arrive at the Palais Jamaï, a lovely old Moroccan palace with a terrace overlooking a beautiful garden, full of orange trees and scented① flowers. Her room was decorated in eastern style, and was full of modern comforts.

Later Hilary enjoyed an excellent dinner and then had coffee outside on the terrace. There she noticed a very old man with a yellow-tinted face and a small beard. The hotel staff served him very attentively, taking away his empty plates immediately and hurrying to his table as soon as he looked up. Hilary wondered who he was, but she was too tired to think about it and went to bed early.

The next morning Hilary sat outside in the sunshine under a red-striped umbrella. It was strange to sit in such a peaceful place, pretending to be a dead woman. As she watched children

---

① scented *adj.* 芬芳的

run up and down the terrace, Hilary couldn't believe that anything unusual was going to happen.

The old man with the yellow face came up to the terrace from the gardens below and sat down at a table nearby. When Hilary ordered a drink, she asked the waiter, 'Who is that old man over there?'

'That, Madame,' the waiter said quietly, 'is Monsieur Aristides. He is enormously rich.' Hilary looked over at the old man, just as he too looked up. They stared at each other for a moment until the old man looked away. Hilary thought that Mr Aristides' eyes looked alive and intelligent.

Later in the afternoon, as Hilary was resting outside, a shadow suddenly appeared on her chair. She looked up, surprised, to see Mr Aristides. He was not looking at Hilary, and when he turned round he accidentally knocked her glass off the table.

'Ah, pardon me, Madame,' Mr Aristides said politely. Hilary smiled and said in French that it did not matter. Mr Aristides then told the waiter to bring her another drink, before he apologized again and went into the restaurant.

When the waiter brought her drink, Hilary asked him if Mr Aristides was alone at the hotel.

The waiter was shocked. 'Oh, no, Madame,' he said. 'Monsieur Aristides is so rich that he never travels alone. He has a personal servant, two secretaries and a driver.' But when she went into the restaurant Hilary noticed that the old man sat by himself.

The afternoon passed very pleasantly. Hilary walked through the beautiful gardens, looking at the oranges and smelling the different flowers. The place was very peaceful, and Hilary wished she could stay for ever. It was strange that she had found peace at last, just when she was starting a dangerous adventure. But perhaps there was no danger and no adventure...

When she went back inside the hotel late in the afternoon, Hilary was surprised to meet Mrs Baker in the lounge. 'I've just arrived by plane,' Mrs Baker explained. 'Trains are so slow, and the people in them aren't always very clean. Now tell me what you've been doing, Mrs Betterton. Have you seen the old town yet?'

'No, I'm afraid I haven't,' said Hilary, smiling. 'I've just been sitting in the sun.'

'Oh, yes, you've just come out of hospital,' said Mrs Baker. 'I suppose you must be tired. I never feel tired. Do you remember Miss Hetherington, the Englishwoman at Casablanca? She'll be arriving here this evening. She prefers to travel by train — or perhaps that's all she can afford. Now I must go and sort out my room — I didn't like the one they first gave me.' Mrs Baker left, energetic as always.

Hilary saw Miss Hetherington in the dining room that evening, and then she and the two new arrivals had coffee together. Miss Hetherington had discovered that a rich Swedish businessman was staying at the hotel with a blonde film star.

'And they're not married,' she said excitedly. 'There's so much of that kind of thing abroad. There's a nice French family at the table by the window, though of course French children are allowed to stay up far too late. Their parents even let them drink *wine*.' She sounded horrified.

Meanwhile, Mrs Baker was making plans for the next day. 'I've been to the old city before,' she said. 'It was very interesting but I was glad I had a guide with me. All those twisting streets — without him I would have become very lost. Of course he took me to a friend's house — they always do — and wanted me to buy lots of souvenirs. I had to be quite firm.'

Miss Hetherington sighed. 'It would be nice to buy souvenirs, but they're so expensive.' she said sadly.

Chapter 7

I

Fortunately Hilary was able to visit the old city of Fez without Miss Hetherington or Mrs Baker, who had gone on a sightseeing trip by car — for which Mrs Baker paid. With her guide, Hilary walked down through the gardens of the hotel until they reached a big door in the wall. And through that door Hilary stepped into another world — the old city of Fez.

Hilary wandered through the narrow, twisting streets, interested in everything she saw. She enjoyed looking around her at the busy life of the Moroccan city. The only annoyance was her guide, who talked all the time, asking her to buy things. 'You look, lady,' he kept saying. 'This man have very nice things, very cheap.'

Hilary walked for what seemed like hours, until finally her guide said, 'I take you to very nice house now, lady. Friends of mine. You have tea and they show you many nice things.' Because she was tired, Hilary allowed herself to be taken to an attractive house outside the city walls. Here she drank mint tea and, to be polite, bought a few small souvenirs.

'Now I take you for a nice drive to see very beautiful views,' said her guide. 'And then back to hotel. But first, this girl will take you to very nice ladies' toilet.'

Smiling a little, Hilary followed the girl to the toilet, which she was pleased to find had running water. But when she had washed her hands Hilary found that she couldn't open the door.

Why had she been locked in? Then she noticed another door in the corner of the room. This door opened easily and Hilary walked into a small room lit by high windows. Sitting on an eastern-style chair was the little Frenchman she had met in the train — Monsieur Henri Laurier.

II

'Good afternoon, Mrs Betterton,' he said.

For a moment Hilary was too surprised to speak. So this — this was it! This was what she had been waiting for. She stepped forward. 'Do you have news for me? Can you help me?'

He nodded. 'On the train, Madame, you were rather stupid. Or perhaps you always talk about the weather.'

The weather? She stared at him. What had he said about the weather? Cold? Fog? Snow?

Snow — that was it. Olive Betterton had talked about snow. What was the silly rhyme she had said? Hilary remembered. *'Snow, snow, beautiful snow! You slip on a lump, and over you go!'* she repeated to Laurier.

'Exactly,' said Laurier. 'Why did you not follow your instructions and say that before?'

'You don't understand,' said Hilary. 'I was in a plane crash and I've been in hospital with concussion. It has affected my memory and I've forgotten a lot of important things.'

'Yes,' said Laurier, 'the plane crash was unfortunate.' His voice was cold. 'But are you now ready to continue your journey?'

'Of course I am,' said Hilary. 'I *must* see my husband...'

He smiled, but not a very pleasant smile. 'You were

questioned by the British authorities,' he said. 'Do you think they suspect you?'

'I don't know,' said Hilary. 'They *seemed* satisfied, but I have the feeling that I'm being followed.'

'We know that,' said Laurier, coldly. 'We are not stupid.'

'I'm sorry,' said Hilary. 'I'm afraid it's me who is stupid.'

'It does not matter if you are stupid, as long as you do as you are told — as long as you obey①.'

'I will obey,' said Hilary quietly.

'Now, Madame, I will give you your instructions,' said Laurier. 'The day after tomorrow you will fly back to Marrakesh. There you will receive a message telling you to go back to England.'

'I am going *back to England*?'

'Please listen — I have not finished. You will book a seat on the plane leaving for Casablanca the next day. Do you understand?'

'I understand,' said Hilary.

'Then please return to your guide — you have been in here long enough. But before you go, I believe that you have become friendly with an American woman and an Englishwoman at your hotel?'

'Yes — is that wrong?'

'No, it fits in with our plans. See if one or other of them will come with you to Marrakesh. Goodbye, Madame.'

Hilary went back to her guide. 'I have very nice car waiting,' he said. 'I take you now for very pleasant drive.'

---

① obey *v.* 遵守

III

'So you're leaving for Marrakesh tomorrow,' said Miss Hetherington. 'You haven't stayed very long in Fez, have you?'

'No,' agreed Hilary, 'but my tickets are booked now and I think it will be too difficult to change them again — there are so many other people travelling.'

'Not English people,' said Miss Hetherington sadly. 'They all seem to be French.'

Hilary smiled faintly. The fact that Morocco was controlled by the French did not seem to matter to Miss Hetherington.

'There are a lot of Germans and Swedish people here, too,' added Mrs Baker, 'and I'm told that that little old man over there is Greek. He seems to be important — or at least the waiters think he is.'

'I wish you two would come to Marrakesh with me,' said Hilary. 'It's been so pleasant talking to you here, and it's very lonely travelling by myself.'

'But I've *been* to Marrakesh,' said Miss Hetherington in a shocked voice.

Mrs Baker, however, seemed interested. 'That's quite a good idea,' she said. 'I'd like to go back to Marrakesh, and I can show you around. I'll go and see if I can arrange it.' She stood up and hurried off with her usual energy.

'That's just like Americans,' said Miss Hetherington, annoyed. 'They always rush from place to place. Sometimes I don't think they know what country they're in.' She picked up her knitting① and said goodbye to Hilary before going upstairs.

---

① knitting *n*. 针织品

Hilary sat alone in the hotel lounge. She was thinking about the future. Now she was going to start her real journey, so she must be very careful and not make any mistakes. She must be Olive Betterton, devoted① to her husband.

Hilary jumped in surprise as she saw the small, wrinkled② face of Mr Aristides suddenly appear before her. He bowed politely and asked if he could sit down. After a moment or two he asked, 'Do you like this country, Madame?'

'I've been here only a short time,' said Hilary, 'but yes, I love it. And the old city of Fez is wonderful.'

'Yes, it is wonderful,' he agreed. 'There everything is dark and secret, shut in behind narrow streets and walls. Do you know what I think of, Madame, when I walk through the streets of Fez?'

'No.'

'I think of that main road into London, the Great West Road. I think of the great factory buildings on each side of the road, brightly lit, so you can clearly see all the people inside as you drive along in your car. There is nothing hidden, there is nothing secret.'

'So you mean,' said Hilary, thoughtfully, 'that you are interested in the contrast between them — Fez and the road in London? Because they are so different?'

Mr Aristides nodded. 'Yes,' he said. 'But although they look so different, the same things happen in both places. There is always cruelty and there is always kindness. One or the other. Sometimes both.' He continued without changing his manner. 'I have been told, Madame, that you were in a very bad plane

---

① devoted *adj.* 全心全意的 ② wrinkled *adj.* 有皱纹的

accident? I envy[①] you.'

Hilary looked at him with astonishment.

'Yes,' he repeated, 'I envy you. You have come close to death, and yet you survived. Do you feel different since then, Madame?'

'Only in a bad way,' said Hilary. 'I had concussion, and so I get headaches and forget things easily.'

'Those things will get better,' said Mr Aristides, with a wave of his hand, 'but you — you have had an adventure of the spirit, have you not?'

'It is true,' said Hilary slowly, thinking of her pile of sleeping pills. 'I have had an adventure of the spirit.'

'I have never had that experience,' said Mr Aristides in a dissatisfied voice. 'So many other things, but not that.' He stood up and bowed politely. 'Goodbye, Madame,' he said, and left Hilary sitting alone once again.

---

① envy *v.* 嫉妒

Chapter 8

'All airports are strangely alike,' thought Hilary, as she waited for the plane to Marrakesh. 'And why do you have to get there much too early?'

They had been sitting in the waiting room for nearly an hour. Mrs Baker, who had decided to come with Hilary, had been talking for the whole time. Now, thankfully, she was talking to two other travellers who were sitting near her. They were both tall young men with fair hair. One was an American with a big friendly smile, and the other was a rather serious-looking Norwegian, who talked slowly in careful English. The American was clearly delighted to find another traveller from his own country.

Mrs Baker turned to Hilary. 'Mr —?' she said. 'I'd like you to meet my friend, Mrs Betterton.'

'My name's Andrew Peters,' said the American. 'My friends call me Andy.'

The other young man stood up and bowed rather stiffly. 'My name is Torquil Ericsson,' he said.

'Now we all know each other,' said Mrs Baker happily.

Suddenly the loudspeaker gave an announcement in French telling them that they could now board the plane. As well as Hilary and Mrs Baker, there were four other passengers — Peters, Ericsson, a tall, thin Frenchman and a stern①-looking nun.

It was a clear, sunny day, good for flying, and Hilary sat

---

① stern *adj*. 苛刻的

back in her seat and looked at her fellow① passengers. Mrs Baker was reading a magazine. Now and then she tapped the shoulder of the fair young American, Peters, who was sitting in front of her. He always turned round with a smile, responding to Mrs Baker's remarks with enthusiasm. 'How friendly Americans are,' thought Hilary. 'Not like the English.'

Sitting across from her was the Norwegian, Torquil Ericsson. As she looked at him, he nodded and offered her his magazine to read. Hilary thanked him and took it.

In the seat behind Ericsson sat the thin Frenchman. His legs were stretched out and he seemed to be asleep. Then Hilary looked behind her at the stern-looking nun, who looked back at Hilary with no expression on her face. She sat very still.

'Six different people,' thought Hilary, 'travelling together for a few hours and then separating, never to meet again...' She closed her eyes and thought again about the instructions she had been given. Why was she going back to England? Didn't they trust her — had she made a mistake? Or was it because she was being watched? To get home she would have to stop in Paris — and Tom Betterton had disappeared in Paris. Was the same thing going to happen to her? At last she grew tired of thinking, and fell asleep.

When she woke up the plane was flying in circles, preparing to land. Hilary looked out of the window, but she couldn't see an airfield below her. Nor could she see any houses or a town — just desert②. This wasn't Marrakesh. Where were they?

The plane landed with a bump, in the middle of nowhere. The pilot asked them all to get out. Had something gone wrong with the plane, Hilary wondered?

---

① fellow *adj.* 面临同种情况的　② desert *n.* 沙漠

Outside, the wind blew cold from the snow-topped mountains in the distance. The pilot asked them to wait, and soon they saw a vehicle moving slowly towards them. It was a big car — a station wagon①.

'But why have we landed here?' asked Hilary. 'What's the matter? Did the engine fail?'

Andy Peters smiled cheerfully. 'I don't think so,' he said. 'But I'm sure that's what they'll say.'

Hilary stared at him, puzzled.

The station wagon arrived and the Moroccan driver got out. Together with the pilot — and with help from Ericsson and Peters — they lifted out a large, heavy crate② from the back of the car. As they went to open it, Mrs Baker led Hilary away. 'Don't watch, my dear. It's never a nice thing to see.' The Frenchman and Peters followed them.

'Are you Dr Barron?' Mrs Baker asked the Frenchman.

'I am.' The Frenchman bowed.

'I'm pleased to meet you,' said Mrs Baker, shaking his hand as if she was welcoming him to a party.

'I don't understand,' said Hilary. 'What's in that crate? Why is it better not to look?'

Andy Peters looked at her — he had a nice face, Hilary thought. 'There are bodies in the crate,' Peters said. 'The pilot told me.'

'Bodies!' She stared at him.

'Oh, they weren't murdered or anything,' he smiled. 'They're dead bodies used for medical research.'

But Hilary still stared. 'I still don't understand,' she said.

'You see, Mrs Betterton, this is where the journey ends,'

---

① station wagon *n*. 旅行轿车　② crate *n*. 大木箱

explained Peters. 'They'll arrange the bodies in the plane and then set it on fire. People will think that another plane has crashed, with no survivors!'

'But why?' said Hilary.

'Don't you know,' said Dr Barron, 'where we are going?'

'Of course she knows,' said Mrs Baker cheerfully. 'But I don't think she expected it to happen quite so soon.'

Hilary said with surprise, 'But you mean — all of us?' She looked round.

'We're fellow-travellers①,' said Peters gently.

The young Norwegian, Torquil Ericsson, nodded in agreement. 'Yes, we are all fellow-travellers,' he said with enthusiasm.

---

① fellow-travellers *n*. 同路人(参见 123 页**文化注释**)

Chapter 9

I

The pilot approached them. 'You must leave now, please,' he said. 'We have much to do, and we are already late.'

Hilary stepped back and nervously put her hand up to her throat. The necklace of pearls① that she was wearing broke under her fingers, and she quickly picked up the loose pearls and put them in her pocket.

They all got into the station wagon, where Hilary sat between Peters and Mrs Baker. 'So — so you are in charge of organizing us all?' Hilary asked Mrs Baker.

'That's right,' Mrs Baker replied. 'It's quite natural for an American woman to travel around a lot.'

Mrs Baker still looked the same, but Hilary thought that she acted differently — she was more efficient, and perhaps more ruthless②.

'The newspapers will say that you were very unlucky, dear,' added Mrs Baker. 'Nearly dying in one plane crash and then being killed so soon in another.'

'Who are these other people?' Hilary asked quietly.

'They're all scientists,' Mrs Baker replied. 'I don't really understand what they all do, but Dr Barron works with viruses③ and diseases, Mr Ericsson is a brilliant physicist and Mr Peters is a nuclear chemist. And Miss Needheim, of course,

---

① pearl *n*. 珍珠 ② ruthless *adj*. 残忍的 ③ virus *n*. 病毒

isn't a nun. She's a German biologist. Me, I'm just the organizer — I don't belong with the scientists.' She laughed. 'That Hetherington woman never had a chance.'

'Miss Hetherington?' said Hilary. 'Was she...?'

Mrs Baker nodded. 'She was following you,' she said. 'But it would have been out of character[①] if she had come back to Marrakesh so soon. She'll tell someone new to follow you from Marrakesh when you arrive. But of course you won't arrive!' She laughed again, just as they heard a sudden loud noise. 'Ah, look! That's the plane.'

They had been driving across the desert, and when Hilary looked back she saw a big yellow glow[②] behind them. The plane had exploded and was on fire.

Andy Peters laughed. 'Six people die when plane to Marrakesh crashes!'

'It's — it's rather frightening,' said Hilary quietly.

'Travelling to an unknown destination[③]?' Peters said. He was serious now. 'Yes, but it's the only way. We're leaving the past behind and are stepping out towards the future.' He spoke with sudden enthusiasm. 'We have to leave the old bad things behind. The new world of science will be clean and clear!'

Hilary took a deep breath. 'That's the kind of thing my husband says,' she replied carefully.

'Your husband?' said Peters. 'Is your husband Tom Betterton?'

Hilary nodded.

'That's great,' said Peters. 'I've never met him, but of course I know about ZE Fission. He worked with Dr

---

① out of character 不符合某人的性格　② glow n. 稳定而微弱的光
③ destination n. 目的地

Mannheim, didn't he? I thought he married Mannheim's daughter.'

'I'm his second wife,' said Hilary, her face a little red. 'He — his — Elsa died in America.'

'I remember now,' said Peters. 'He went to work in England but he disappeared from Paris. Everything is very well organized.'

Hilary agreed with him. Secretly she was worried. There was no trail① for anyone to follow, and all the codes② and signs she had learned were now useless. She was indeed on her way to an unknown destination, and there was nothing to show where she had gone. All there was to find was a burnt plane and six dead bodies. Would Jessop guess that she wasn't dead?

They drove on. Night fell and still they drove on through the desert. The ground was rough and bumpy, and they were obviously not on a main road.

For a long time Hilary sat still, thoughts turning in her head, but at last she was too tired to stay awake any longer. She let her eyes close and fell into an uneasy sleep.

II

The car had stopped. 'Wake up,' Peters said gently to Hilary. 'We've arrived somewhere.'

Everyone got out of the station wagon, tired and stiff. It was still dark, but in front of them they could see a house surrounded by palm trees, and Hilary could see the lights from a village in the distance. Inside the house they were greeted by two laughing local Moroccan women, who led them upstairs.

---

① trail *n*. 痕迹 ② code *n*. 密码

The men went to one room, while the three women were taken into a small room with three mattresses① on the floor.

'My body's so stiff,' complained Mrs Baker. 'That car was very uncomfortable on that bumpy road.'

'Discomfort does not matter,' said Miss Needheim, the nun. Her voice was harsh② and confident and she spoke English well, though with a strong foreign accent. 'It is weakness. When you are strong, nothing is too much to suffer.'

'Well, all I want now is a comfortable bed,' said Mrs Baker, yawning. 'And I'm sure that journey hasn't helped your concussion, has it, Mrs Betterton?'

'No, it hasn't,' Hilary agreed.

'They'll bring us something to eat soon,' said Mrs Baker, 'and then I'll give you some medicine to help your headache.'

Sure enough, the two local women soon brought them a tray of food and some water to wash with. They stood and looked at Hilary's European clothes, laughing and talking to each other, until Mrs Baker waved them away.

'Silly things,' said Mrs Baker, 'I suppose all they are interested in is clothes and babies.'

'It is all they are fit for,' said Miss Needheim. 'They are slaves③, and their only use is to serve.'

'That's very unfair,' said Hilary, annoyed by the woman's attitude.

'I only speak the truth. There are a few people who rule — and there are many who serve.'

'But surely ...'

Mrs Baker interrupted. 'It is time to rest now,' she said firmly, and after they had eaten some food and washed, the

---

① mattress *n*. 床垫　② harsh *adj*. 严厉的　③ slave *n*. 奴隶

three women lay down to sleep.

They slept late the next day, and when they woke up, Mrs Baker gave them some Moroccan clothes to wear. She explained that they had to leave their European clothes behind.

Now that Miss Needheim was no longer dressed as a nun, Hilary could see her properly. The German woman was about thirty-three and looked very neat. But her pale face and cold eyes were not attractive. She was arrogant①, and acted as if Hilary and Mrs Baker were not good enough to talk to her. Hilary much preferred the laughing local women.

And Mrs Baker — she was still talking normally about everyday things, but Hilary now realized that the American woman was just like an actor playing a part. She had no idea what Mrs Baker was really thinking or feeling.

In the evening they carried on their journey, this time in an open touring② car. Everyone was wearing Moroccan clothes: the men in long white robes③ and the women with their faces hidden. Again, they drove all through the night, and stopped for breakfast when the sun came up.

'How are you feeling, Mrs Betterton?' asked Andy Peters.

'I feel as if I'm in a dream,' said Hilary. 'Where are we?'

'I don't know,' he replied. 'All I know is that we're in the desert. And in the desert we won't leave a trail behind us. Each part of our journey is separate — a plane that crashes, a station wagon and now a touring car of Moroccans, which is a common sight on the road.'

'But where are we going?' said Hilary.

'We'll find out soon,' said Dr Barron as he joined them. 'In the Western world we always want to know things *now*. We

---

① arrogant *adj.* 傲慢的　② touring *adj.* 游览的　③ robe *n.* 长袍

think about tomorrow rather than today. But life is too short. There is so much to achieve and there is not enough time. I need more time for my work!' he said with passion. 'And I need freedom — freedom from fools who constantly interrupt me and my work!'

'You work with viruses, don't you, Dr Barron?' Peters asked.

'Yes, I work with diseases. And to work properly, I need patience, and a lot of money for equipment. With that, I can achieve anything!'

'Can you achieve happiness?' asked Hilary with a smile.

He smiled back, suddenly human again. 'Ah, you are a woman, Madame. It is women who ask always for happiness.'

'The happiness of one person does not matter,' said Peters seriously. 'There must be happiness for *all* people! Science should be used to help everyone, and it should be shared, not controlled by one country or another.'

'Yes!' said Ericsson, who had just joined them, 'you are right. But the scientists must be the masters — they are the only people who matter. They must control and rule the slaves.'

Hilary walked a little way away from the group, and after a few minutes, Peters followed her.

'You look a bit scared,' he said with a laugh.

'I think I am,' said Hilary. 'Of course I'm not a scientist, and I'm not very clever like the rest of you. I'm only a woman, looking for happiness.'

'And what's wrong with that?' said Peters. Then he asked, in a lower voice, 'Why exactly are you here? Do you love your husband so much? Or do you share his views?'

Hilary avoided giving a direct answer. 'Have you noticed that all our fellow-travellers have very different views?'

Peters thought for a moment. 'I do believe you're right,' he said.

'Dr Barron is only interested in his work,' said Hilary, 'while Helga Needheim talks about slaves, and so does Torquil Ericsson — they are like mad scientists in a film!'

'And I believe in freedom for all,' said Peters. 'You're a loving wife, and Mrs Baker — well, I think she's just doing this for the money.'

'She seems so ordinary,' said Hilary, 'and yet she's mixed up in all this.' She shivered suddenly.

'Are you cold?' asked Peters. 'Let's move around for a bit.'

As they walked up and down, Peters suddenly picked up something from the ground.

'Is this yours?' he said.

'Oh, yes,' Hilary replied. 'It's a pearl from my necklace. I broke it the other day — it seems a long time ago now.' She took the pearl from Peters.

'Not real pearls, I hope.'

'No, of course not,' smiled Hilary.

Peters offered her a cigarette. As she took one, Hilary said, 'What a strange cigarette case. It's very heavy.'

'It's made of lead①, that's why,' Peters explained. 'It's a war souvenir — made from a bomb that tried to blow me up. But let's not talk about the war — let's talk about tomorrow.'

'But what can we talk about?' asked Hilary. 'Nobody's told me anything. Are we... ?'

Peters interrupted her. 'You don't need to *know*. You just need to do what you're told and go where you're told. You need to obey.'

---

① lead *n.* 铅

With sudden passion Hilary said, 'And do you like being given orders and told what to do?'

'If it is necessary, yes,' he replied. 'And it *is* necessary. We must have a new world, a peaceful world — a world with order and discipline①!'

'Is that possible?'

'Anything's better than the mess② we live in — don't you agree?'

Hilary was tired and lonely. She wanted to say, 'What's so wrong with the world we live in? Surely it's better to have a world where there is kindness and independence③ — even if it is a mess — rather than an ordered world with no pity or understanding or sympathy!'

But she stopped herself in time. 'You're right,' she said. 'I'm just tired. I'll do what I'm told. I will obey.'

Andy Peters smiled. 'That's better,' he said.

---

① discipline *n.* 纪律 ② mess *n.* 杂乱 ③ independence *n.* 独立

Chapter 10

As their journey continued, Hilary felt that she was living in a dream, as if she really was becoming Olive Betterton. Every day she became more and more serious and intense①, like her companions. All five were so different, but slowly Hilary became a little frightened of all of them. They were all so determined and focused on one thing — they all had one thing that they believed in passionately, above all else.

Dr Barron cared only about his work. He was desperate for knowledge, to find things out. But he never asked himself *why*. It was the process of discovery that interested him. He told Hilary once that he had found a virus with the power to destroy a whole country, but he was interested in *how* it would destroy — he did not seem to think about the people the virus would kill.

She didn't like Helga Needheim at all, because the woman was so very arrogant. Hilary liked Peters but sometimes he frightened her by the almost fanatical② way he talked. She said to him once, 'You don't want to create a new world, do you? You just want to destroy the old one. There's hate in you. I can feel it.'

Torquil Ericsson was more of a puzzle. He liked to dream of how he wanted the world to be. 'We must take over the world,' he said gently, 'so we — the people with brains — can rule. That is all that matters.'

They are all mad, Hilary thought, but in different ways.

---

① intense *adj.* 激烈的 ② fanatical *adj.* 狂热的

Then she looked at Mrs Baker. She wasn't interested in ruling the world. She didn't seem to believe in anything at all — except perhaps money.

At the end of the third day of travelling, they arrived at a small town and slept in a local hotel for the night. Very early the next morning they were given European clothes to wear and drove to an airfield. There they boarded a small plane and flew for hours. Hilary looked out of the window and saw mountains through the clouds, but she had no idea where they were.

In the early afternoon, the plane landed on flat ground surrounded by mountains. They had arrived at a private airfield where there were two big cars waiting for them.

'This is where the journey ends,' said Mrs Baker cheerfully. 'The cars will be ready soon.'

Hilary stared at her. 'But we haven't crossed the sea,' she said in surprise.

'Did you expect to?' Mrs Baker seemed amused.

'But where are we — what part of the world, I mean?'

'Oh, that's no secret now. This is a lonely place in the High Atlas mountains. We're still in Morocco.' Mrs Baker looked at her watch. 'Well, goodbye, everyone,' she said. 'This is where I leave you.'

'Are you going back to Marrakesh?' asked Hilary.

'No,' said Mrs Baker, 'I can't do that. I'm supposed to have died in a plane crash. I'm going to organize people somewhere else now.'

'But what if someone recognizes you?' Hilary asked.

'They won't,' said Mrs Baker. 'I have a new passport now. My sister, Mrs Baker, died in a plane crash — we look very alike. And no one I met knows me that well,' she added. 'To them I'm just another travelling American.'

'It's strange,' Hilary said, 'that even after travelling with you for so long I don't know you very well. I don't even know which part of America you're from.'

'That doesn't matter,' said Mrs Baker. 'I can never go back there.' For a moment her face looked angry and spiteful①. Then she said cheerfully, 'Goodbye, Mrs Betterton. I hope you see your husband soon.'

Hilary watched as Mrs Baker said goodbye to the others before going back to the plane. Hilary shivered. Mrs Baker was her last link② with the outside world. Peters, standing near her, seemed to know what she was thinking.

'This is the place of no return,' he said quietly.

'Do you want to go back, Madame?' asked Dr Barron. 'Back to the world you have left?'

'Could I go if I wanted to?' asked Hilary.

'I don't know,' said Peters. 'Shall I ask Mrs Baker before she leaves?'

'Of course not,' said Hilary sharply.

'This is no place for women who are weak,' said Helga Needheim scornfully③.

'She is not weak,' said Dr Barron softly. 'She asks herself questions as any intelligent woman would do.' But Helga Needheim ignored the Frenchman, while Ericsson asked, 'When you have reached freedom, how can you think of going back?'

'But if you can't go back, or choose to go back,' argued Hilary, 'then it is not freedom!'

They were interrupted by one of the drivers telling them that the cars were ready. Hilary sat in the front next to the driver,

---

① spiteful *adj.* 恶意的 ② link *n.* 联系 ③ scornfully *adv.* 轻蔑地

and talked to him in French as they drove along.

'How long will it take us?' she asked.

'To get to the hospital? About two hours, Madame.'

Hilary was surprised at the driver's words. 'Tell me about the hospital,' she said.

'Ah, Madame, it is a wonderful place,' the driver said with enthusiasm. 'It has all the most modern equipment and many doctors come to visit and are very impressed① by the new treatments. Before, such people had to live completely separate and were left to die, but now they have a chance of a cure②.'

'It seems a lonely place to have a hospital,' said Hilary.

'Ah, Madame, but it has to be lonely — the authorities insist,' said the driver. 'See, over there,' he pointed. 'That is where we are going.'

In the distance Hilary saw a low range of mountains, and at the bottom of one of the mountains was a long white building.

'It is a wonderful place,' said the driver again. 'So much money has been spent. Our patron③ is one of the richest men in the world, and here he has done so much to help human suffering.'

At last the car stopped outside some huge iron gates. 'You must walk from here, Madame,' explained the driver. As the travellers got out of the car, the big gates opened and a tall, dark-skinned man wearing long white robes bowed and asked them to enter.

As they walked through the gates they saw a large courtyard with a tall wire fence, where people were walking up and down. As these people turned to look at the new arrivals,

---

① impressed *adj.* (对……)钦佩的　② cure *n.* 治疗　③ patron *n.* 赞助人

Hilary gasped in horror.

  'But they're lepers[①]!' she exclaimed. '*Lepers*!'

---

① leper *n.* 麻风病患者

Chapter 11

The huge iron gates closed firmly behind the travellers. To Hilary this felt like the end — there was no way out. Now she was alone, and soon she would be discovered...

She had known all day that this moment would come. Jessop had said that if she got this far, she would have protection, but if she was supposed to rely on Miss Hetherington, that plan had failed. And what, thought Hilary, could Miss Hetherington have done to help her now?

Now that she was close to discovery and death, Hilary realized that she no longer wanted to die. She was enjoying life again. She could think of Nigel and Brenda with sadness and pity, not cold lifeless despair. 'I'm alive again at last,' thought Hilary. 'But now I'm trapped① — like a rat in a trap. Can I find a way out?'

She had often thought about what would happen when she met Tom Betterton. He would say, 'That's not my wife —' and everyone would know she was a spy②. So what could she do?

Perhaps she could speak first? She could say, 'Who are you? *You're* not my husband!' If she pretended well enough, would they believe her? If they did believe her, it would be bad for Betterton. But if he was a traitor③ who had sold his country's secrets, didn't he deserve it? This was the only thing she could think of that was worth trying.

Hilary had been thinking all this as she walked along. She

---

① trapped *adj.* 被困的 ② spy *n.* 间谍 ③ traitor *n.* 叛徒

felt a little faint but tried hard to focus on what was happening. They were being welcomed by a big handsome man, who spoke a few words to everyone in their own language.

To Hilary, he said, 'Ah, Mrs Betterton, welcome, after your long and difficult journey. Your husband is waiting for you, very excited.' He smiled, though Hilary noticed that his eyes stayed cold. 'You must be longing① to see him.'

Hilary suddenly felt faint again, and Andy Peters put out an arm and steadied her as she swayed②. 'Perhaps you don't know,' he said, 'that Mrs Betterton was in a plane crash and has concussion. The journey has been hard for her — she should lie down.'

Hilary thought how kind he was, and she held on to his arm for support. She wanted to faint, to lie down — anything to delay the moment of discovery! But Betterton would come to see her — any husband would — and he would realize that she was not his wife.

Then suddenly Hilary's courage returned. She stood up straight and lifted her head. She would be brave. She would say to Betterton, 'I'm sorry, but your wife is dead. I promised to reach you and give you her final message. I agree with your views and I want to help.'

It wasn't a very convincing story — and it didn't explain things like her fake③ passport. 'But sometimes,' thought Hilary, 'if you tell lies with enough confidence, people do believe you. I have to try.'

'Oh, no. I must see Tom,' she said. 'I must see him now — please.'

'Of course, Mrs Betterton,' said the big man. 'I'll take you

---

① long *v.* 渴望　② sway *v.* 摇摆　③ fake *adj.* 假的

to him now. Please follow me.'

As she walked away, Hilary looked over her shoulder. Andy Peters was watching her, and his face looked puzzled and unhappy. 'He has realized something is wrong,' she thought, 'but he doesn't know what it is.' Hilary shivered. She might never see him again.

The big man was talking cheerfully. 'This way, Mrs Betterton. Our buildings are rather confusing at first. There are so many white corridors that all look the same.'

'It's all a little strange — and rather frightening,' said Hilary. 'The lepers...'

'Yes, yes, of course. They do upset our new arrivals. But you'll get used to them. By the way, my name is Van Heidem — Dr Paul Van Heidem. We're nearly there now.'

Nearly there — nearly there... They went down another white corridor and Van Heidem finally stopped at a door, knocked and opened it.

'Ah, Betterton,' he said. 'Here's your wife — at last!' Hilary walked in bravely, holding her head up.

A very good-looking man with fair hair stood by the window. Hilary was surprised — this man did not look like the photograph of Tom Betterton. She decided to take a risk.

She stepped forward, and then back. 'But — that isn't Tom,' she said. 'That isn't my husband...' She thought she sounded convincing.

And then Tom Betterton laughed. 'It must be good,' he said to Van Heidem, 'if even my own wife doesn't recognize me!'

He quickly walked over to Hilary and held her tightly in his arms. 'Olive, darling, it's really me — Tom — even if my face has changed a little.' Then Hilary heard him whisper, 'Be careful. Danger.'

Betterton looked at her face before holding her again. 'Darling, it's been so long since I've seen you,' he continued. 'But you're here at last!' Hilary felt his fingers pressing hard into her back, as if giving her a warning. 'I still can't believe you're here,' he said, with an excited little laugh. 'But you know it's me now, don't you?'

Hilary didn't understand it — couldn't understand it. But she gratefully tried to play her part. 'Tom!' she said, 'Oh, Tom — but what...'

'I've had plastic surgery①,' he explained, 'to change my face.' He kissed her lightly.

'It's been so long,' said Hilary, 'and I —' she swayed a little. 'I — please, can I sit down?'

'Of course, darling,' said Betterton, getting her a chair. 'You've had such a bad time — and that plane crash! — I'm so glad you're all right!'

'So they knew about the plane crash,' thought Hilary. 'That means they must be in communication with the outside world.'

'The concussion has affected my memory,' she said. 'I forget things and get confused. And then when I finally see you, you look like a total stranger! It's a bit much for me.'

'You just need to rest for a while, darling,' said Betterton.

Van Heidem moved towards the door. 'I will leave you alone now,' he said. 'Perhaps later, Betterton, you will bring your wife to the Registry②?' He went out and shut the door.

Immediately Betterton dropped on his knees in front of Hilary and rested his face on her shoulder.

'Darling, darling,' he said out loud. Then Hilary heard him whisper, 'Keep going. They might be listening.' Hilary could

---

① plastic surgery n. 整形手术　② registry n. 登记处

feel his fear and uneasiness. She looked at him and saw a good-looking man of about thirty, who was badly frightened. He looked as if he was close to a nervous collapse①.

Now that the immediate danger was over, Hilary began to enjoy playing her part. She must *be* Olive Betterton — act and feel just as Olive would. And the situation was so unreal she didn't feel as if she *was* Hilary Craven any more.

She remembered the details she had learned with Jessop. 'It seems such a long time since we lived at our house, Firbank,' she said. 'Whiskers — do you remember my cat, Whiskers? She had kittens just after you went away. It's strange that there are so many silly little things you don't even know about.'

'I know,' said Betterton. 'That was the old life. Here we'll begin a new life.'

'And it's all right here? You're happy?' Hilary was sure a loving wife would ask this.

'It's wonderful.' Tom Betterton lifted his head. His unhappy frightened eyes looked out of a smiling, confident face. 'The working conditions are perfect. There's everything you could ever want here.'

'And is it really a leper colony②?'

'Oh, yes. The doctors here are researching the disease. But it's just a disguise, a cover.'

'I see.' Hilary looked round. 'Is this our apartment?'

'Yes. Sitting room, bathroom and bedroom — I'll show you.'

Hilary walked through the apartment. Everything was of good quality and very comfortable. There was a lot of space in the cupboards.

---

① collapse *n*. 崩溃 ② colony *n*. 聚居区

'I don't know what I'll put in here,' she said with a laugh. 'I didn't bring anything with me.'

'Don't worry,' said Tom. 'You can get anything you want here. There's no need to go outside ever again.'

He said the words lightly, but Hilary heard the despair in his voice. No need to go outside ever again. They were in a cage — trapped!

And were they being spied on, too? Was someone listening and watching them now? Tom Betterton thought so, but was he right? Or was he in such a nervous state that he was imagining things? Was this what happened to you when you lived in a cage?

'Would you like to lie down — to rest?' Tom asked.

'No —' Hilary hesitated. 'No, I don't think so.'

'Then perhaps you had better come with me to the Registry.'

'What's the Registry?'

'It's where they record everything about you — health, blood pressure①, likes, dislikes — everything. It's very well organized here.'

'I knew it would be,' said Hilary. She tried to speak with real enthusiasm.

Tom Betterton kissed her again. 'Keep going,' he whispered. Out loud he said, 'And now, let's go to the Registry.'

---

① blood pressure n. 血压

Chapter 12

The Registry was managed by a strict-looking Swiss woman, who wore glasses and had an unattractive hair style. 'Ah,' she said when they arrived, 'you've brought Mrs Betterton.' As Hilary sat down, the woman took out a lot of forms and started to write. Tom Betterton said awkwardly, 'I'll leave you, Olive,' and shut the door behind him.

'Now then,' said the woman seriously, 'Tell me your full name, please. Age. Where you were born. Parent's names. Any serious illnesses. Hobbies. List of any jobs held. Degrees① from any university. What you like to eat and drink.' The questions went on and on. Hilary answered almost without thinking, glad that she was so well prepared about Olive's life.

When they finally finished, Hilary was given a thorough medical examination. And then she saw Dr Rubec, a tall, sad-looking Swiss man of about forty, for intelligence and personality tests.

Hilary was nervous about the tests, but they seemed to be routine. When they were over, Dr Rubec said, 'Please do not think I am being rude, Madame, when I say that it is a pleasure to deal with someone who is not a genius②.'

Hilary laughed. 'Oh, I'm certainly not a genius,' she said.

'You are fortunate,' said Dr Rubec. 'It will make your life here much easier. I mostly see very sensitive intellectual people here — but they are not always emotionally stable③. Real scientists are not cool and calm, like they are in books. You would

---

① degree *n.* 学位　② genius *n.* 天才　③ stable *adj.* 稳定的

not believe the arguments and the jealousies that I have to deal with here!'

Next Hilary was taken to the dress department, which was run by Mademoiselle La Roche. The Frenchwoman was not what Hilary was expecting — she used to work in a famous Paris fashion house where rich women bought their clothes, and was interested in purely feminine things.

'I am delighted to meet you, Madame,' she said to Hilary. 'I'm sure you are tired after your journey, so perhaps today you should just select a few essential items.'

'I'd like that,' said Hilary. 'All I own now is a toothbrush.'

Mademoiselle La Roche laughed and took Hilary into a large room with many cupboards filled with clothes of every different size and style. There were also endless underclothes, shoes, makeup and toiletries. Hilary chose a few things from the huge selection, and one of the assistants was told to take everything to her apartment.

'It will be a pleasure to help you choose some more clothes later, when you are more rested,' said Mademoiselle La Roche. 'You are not like scientific ladies — they do not care what they wear or what they look like! Ah, here is Miss Jennson.'

A thin girl with dark hair and glasses had entered the dress department. After she had introduced herself, Miss Jennson said, 'If you've finished here now, Mrs Betterton, I will take you back to Dr Van Heidem. He is the Deputy Director, in charge of managing the Unit[①].' Hilary followed Miss Jennson to Van Heidem's office.

'So, Mrs Betterton,' said Van Heidem, when Hilary arrived. 'I'm sure you are glad to see your husband again. I

---

① unit n. 单位

hope you'll be very happy here.'

'Thank you.' Hilary sat down.

'Do you want to ask me any questions?' the doctor said.

Hilary laughed. 'I have so many questions to ask that I don't know where to begin.'

'Oh, I understand,' he said. 'But my advice is not to ask anything. Just take some time to adapt① and see what happens. That's the best thing to do.'

'But I know so little,' said Hilary. 'It's all so — so unexpected.'

'Yes,' Van Heidem laughed. 'Our desert home is quite a surprise to most people. We don't tell anyone about it before they get here. But we do our best to make everyone comfortable. And if there's anything you need — any particular books or music, for example — just ask.'

After a pause, he continued, 'It usually takes people a few weeks to get used to living here — especially wives. Sometimes wives take time to make new friends.'

'And do we stay here? Or do we move on to somewhere else?'

Van Heidem became rather vague. 'There are possibilities,' he said. 'It depends on your husband. But let's not talk about that now.'

'Can I go out at all?' asked Hilary. 'I mean, go outside the gates?'

'I am often asked that question,' said Van Heidem. His voice was kind. 'But our Unit is a world in itself — it has everything you need. And outside there is only desert.' He smiled. 'After a while, Mrs Betterton, you won't want to go

---

① adapt *v.* 适应

out. You won't want to go back to the bad old world you have left behind.'

Chapter 13

Hilary was back in her apartment. The clothes she had chosen had arrived and she put them away in the wardrobe.

'I went to see the Deputy Director,' Hilary told Betterton.

'Yes, he manages the Unit,' said Betterton. 'But it's the Director who's really in charge.' They spoke carefully, in case someone was listening. 'We don't see the Director very often, though he sometimes gives a speech①. He's very inspiring②.' He looked at his watch. 'We should go down to dinner now, if you're ready.' He spoke as though they were staying in a hotel.

Hilary was wearing a grey-green dress that she had chosen earlier, which looked very attractive with her red hair. They went down the stairs and along several corridors until they reached a large dining room. Miss Jennson showed them to their table, where Andy Peters and Ericsson were already sitting.

Hilary introduced her 'husband' to the two men. They sat down, and were soon joined by another couple, who Betterton introduced as Dr Simon Murchison and his wife Bianca. 'Simon and I work together,' he explained.

Simon Murchison was a thin, pale young man, and his wife Bianca had dark hair and came from Italy. 'Tomorrow,' she said to Hilary, 'I will show you around. Are you a scientist, too?'

'I'm afraid not,' said Hilary. 'I used to work as a secretary.'

'Then perhaps you can help me organize some events here,' suggested Bianca.

---

① speech *n*. 演说 ② inspiring *adj*. 启发灵感的

Hilary was quick to agree to this plan. Then Andy Peters said, 'I feel like a new boy at school. I'll be glad to start work.'

'It's a wonderful place to work,' said Simon Murchison with enthusiasm. 'No interruptions and everything you need.'

'What exactly are you working on?' asked Andy Peters.

All the men started talking about scientific things that Hilary didn't understand. She spoke for a while to Bianca Murchison, who told her about some of the social activities. 'You can play card games, and there is a cinema and sometimes dancing. And there is tennis and squash.'

'I don't really want to do anything else tonight,' said Hilary, yawning. 'I just want to go to bed.'

'Yes, dear,' said Tom Betterton. 'You need a good night's rest after your tiring journey. But do come up to the roof garden for a while — the air is wonderful at night.'

They went up in a lift operated by a tall dark-skinned man wearing white robes. To Hilary's surprise, the roof garden was beautiful — like a fairy story from the book, *Arabian Nights*. There was the sound of water, tall palm trees and lots of green plants. It must have cost a lot of money to create such a beautiful green garden in the desert.

Hilary and Betterton walked around the garden, and gradually all the other people who had been enjoying the night air went back inside. The air was cold and Hilary could see the stars as they sat down, alone at last.

'Now tell me,' said Betterton in a low, nervous voice. 'Who are you?'

Hilary looked at him. Before she answered she had a question of her own. 'Why did you say I was your wife?'

'I don't know — I was stupid. I thought perhaps you had

come to get me out of here.'

'So you want to get out of here?'

'Of course I do! Do you need to ask?'

'Did you know you were coming here?' asked Hilary.

'I didn't know I was coming to Africa, but I knew what I was doing, and came willingly — I wasn't kidnapped. I believed in sharing information with other scientists — and I believed in peace and freedom for everyone.'

Tom Betterton laughed bitterly①. 'But there's no freedom here,' he said. 'I'm always watched and spied on... or am I? Perhaps I'm imagining things. Why should they bother? I can't leave or get away — it's like a prison!'

'So it isn't how you imagined it?' Hilary asked.

'It is in some ways. The working conditions are perfect and there's everything you need. But you're still in prison.'

'I know,' agreed Hilary. 'It was horrible when the gates closed behind us today.'

'So now answer my question,' said Betterton. 'Why are you here, pretending to be Olive? Where *is* Olive?'

'Olive —' Hilary stopped, trying to think of the right words.

'What's happened to her? What are you trying to say?'

'I'm sorry, so sorry,' said Hilary, looking at his nervous face, 'but your wife is dead. She was in a plane crash and died two days later.'

Betterton stared straight ahead of him. He didn't show any emotion. 'So Olive's dead? I see...'

There was a long silence. Then he turned to her. 'So Olive's dead,' he said again. 'But why are *you* here?'

---

① bitterly *adv.* 令人不快地

Hilary was ready for this question. Betterton thought she had come to help him escape, but that wasn't true. She was a spy, here to get information — and now she, too, was a prisoner. But she wasn't going to tell him that — he was too nervous and frightened to keep a secret.

'I was at the hospital with your wife when she died. She wanted to tell you something, so I said I would try to reach you.' As Betterton frowned, Hilary hurried on before he could realize how weak her story was.

'I agree with your ideas,' she said, 'I, too, want peace and freedom. And with my red hair — well, it seemed worth trying.'

'Yes,' he said. 'Your hair's exactly like Olive's.'

'And your wife was so desperate to tell you something — to tell you to be careful — very careful — that you were in danger — from someone called Boris.'

'Boris? Boris Glydr?'

'Yes, do you know him?'

'I've never met him,' said Betterton, 'He's my first wife's cousin. Had Olive seen him? What did he say to her?'

'I don't know. That's all she said. And — oh yes — she said that she couldn't believe it.'

'Believe what?'

'I don't know,' said Hilary. 'You see — she was dying...'

An expression of pain crossed Betterton's face. 'I know you say she's dead, but at the moment I can't really believe it. But what did she mean, about Boris? How can he be dangerous to me *here*?'

'I don't know,' Hilary said again.

There was silence for a moment.

'Oh well, it doesn't matter,' said Betterton. 'We can't

escape.'

'Oh yes, we can,' said Hilary. 'We'll find a way.'

He stared at her. 'You have no idea how hard it would be.'

'There's always a way,' said Hilary confidently. 'We just need time and a good plan.'

'Time?' he said. 'I don't *have* time. I can't work properly here. I can't *think*. They want new and original work — and I just can't do it. It's driving me mad. I'm no use to them like this — they'll kill me.'

'Oh, no!'

'Yes, they will. The only thing that's saved me is that I've had lots of plastic surgery, and I needed time to recover①. But that's finished now.'

'But why did you have plastic surgery at all?'

'For my own safety,' said Betterton. 'The police are looking for me — they want to arrest② me.'

'You mean,' said Hilary, 'because you sold secrets?'

He wouldn't look at her. 'I didn't sell anything. I *gave* them what they wanted. I wanted to share all my scientific knowledge. Don't you understand?'

Hilary thought that she did understand. Andy Peters and Torquil Ericsson would do the same. They would betray their country because they believed that sharing their knowledge would create a better world.

Betterton looked round him nervously. 'Everyone's gone,' he said. 'We should go back down.'

Hilary stood up. 'I've just arrived,' she said. 'They'll understand that we want to be alone.'

'We'll have to go on pretending,' Betterton said awkwardly.

---

① recover *v.* 恢复　② arrest *v.* 逮捕

'That you're my wife, I mean.' He stopped, embarrassed.

Hilary looked at Tom standing in front of her. 'How handsome he is,' thought Hilary. 'But I'm not at all attracted to him.'

'Don't worry,' she said cheerfully. 'The most important thing is to get out of here.'

Chapter 14

In a hotel room in Marrakesh, Jessop was talking to Miss Hetherington. This woman looked the same as the Miss Hetherington that Hilary had known, but she behaved very differently. Now she was confident and positive, and seemed much younger. The third person in the room was a dark-haired, solid-looking Frenchman called Leblanc.

Janet Hetherington was telling Jessop about the people that Hilary — as Olive Betterton — had talked to when they were in Fez. 'There was Mrs Baker, who I had already met at Casablanca,' she said. 'I still can't decide about her. She was friendly with Olive Betterton, but Americans travelling abroad often are friendly. And she was on the plane, too.'

'Yes, what do you think about this plane crash, Leblanc?' said Jessop, turning towards the Frenchman.

'We don't know why the plane crashed,' the Frenchman replied, 'but everyone on board was killed.'

'What do you know about the pilot?' asked Jessop.

'Only that he was young and was a good pilot,' said Leblanc. 'And badly paid.' He paused. 'But there were seven bodies. They were badly burned and couldn't be identified — but there were still seven bodies.'

Jessop turned back to Janet Hetherington. 'Did Mrs Betterton speak to anyone else?'

'She did talk to one of the waiters — and Mr Aristides,' she replied.

'Ah,' said Leblanc, 'Mr Aristides, one of the richest men in the world. And what does he do with all that money? He shuts himself away in a castle in Spain and collects, so they say, Chinese pottery①.'

'Mrs Betterton also visited the old town of Fez with one of the guides,' said Miss Hetherington. 'Someone may have contacted her then.'

'And she suddenly decided to go to Marrakesh,' said Jessop thoughtfully.

'Not suddenly,' said Miss Hetherington. 'Her tickets were already booked.'

'I mean Mrs Baker, not Mrs Betterton,' explained Jessop. 'Mrs Baker suddenly decided to go to Marrakesh. And surely it's strange that Olive Betterton was involved in two plane crashes?' He paused. 'Here's another idea — perhaps the crash was faked.'

Leblanc looked interested. 'It could be done, yes,' he said. 'They could land the plane and set it on fire. But the bodies — there were still seven badly burned bodies on that plane.'

'I know,' said Jessop, 'that's the problem. And there's no trail to follow.'

'I have people searching the area where the plane crashed,' said Leblanc. 'It's a very lonely place. The plane was off its course — flying in the wrong direction.'

'I'm sure that's important,' Jessop said. 'Let's look at the passenger list again.'

The Frenchman gave the list to Jessop and they both examined it carefully.

'Mrs Baker, American. Mrs Betterton, English. Torquil Ericsson, Norwegian. I've heard his name before,' said Jessop, frowning. 'I'm sure he's a scientist of some sort.'

---

① pottery *n.* 陶器

'Then there is a nun, Sister Marie,' said Leblanc. 'And Andrew Peters, American, and Dr Barron, an expert on diseases.'

'That all fits in with what we're looking for,' said Jessop.

The telephone on the table rang and Leblanc answered it. 'Ah, yes,' he said. 'Send them in.' He turned to Jessop. 'My men have found something!' he said with excitement.

A few moments later two men entered the room — a Frenchman and a local Moroccan man. 'I told the local people that there was a reward① if they found anything,' the first man said to Leblanc. 'And this man has found something important.'

The Moroccan took a small object from underneath his white robes. It was a large pearl. Jessop took the pearl and looked at it closely with a magnifying glass.

'Yes! The mark is there,' he said with excitement. 'Good girl — she did it!'

Leblanc was questioning the Moroccan in Arabic. He turned to Jessop. 'This pearl was found nearly half a mile from the burning plane.'

'That means,' said Jessop, 'that Olive Betterton survived the plane crash, and though seven burnt bodies were found, one of them was definitely not hers.'

'I will tell my men to search a bigger area now,' said Leblanc. 'And this man here will get a big reward. When the other local people hear about it, they will look very carefully for these pearls. I just hope,' he added thoughtfully, 'that her fellow-travellers didn't realize what she was doing.'

'Why should they?' asked Jessop. 'Olive Betterton has broken her necklace and a few pearls fell out of her pocket. It isn't suspicious.'

---

① reward n. 奖励

Leblanc looked at the passenger list again. 'Mrs Baker, American. Mrs Betterton, English. Torquil Ericsson, Norwegian — a scientist. We know nothing about him. There is a nun, Sister Marie — a good disguise, perhaps, and Andrew Peters, a nuclear chemist, also American. Last there is Dr Barron — a famous doctor, I believe. All these people have been cleverly brought together to travel in that plane — which is later found on fire with seven dead bodies inside. It is amazing! I wonder how they did it?'

'I don't know,' said Jessop, 'but putting the bodies there was very convincing. But now — because of the pearl — we know that six or seven people in that plane have started a new journey.'

'We should move to a hotel nearer where the plane crashed,' said Leblanc, 'in case other evidence① is found nearby.'

Over the next few days Jessop and Leblanc worked very hard, calculating how far a car could travel from where the plane crashed in each direction, and where it would stop. There were lots of false trails, but at last they got results.

'We have found something,' Leblanc told Jessop. 'A pearl was found in a local man's house. He was paid a great deal of money not to tell anyone that six people stayed the night there. And children in a local village nearby have found two more pearls. So now we know which direction they went in.'

'That's good news,' said Jessop.

'There is more, my friend,' said Leblanc. 'A local man saw a car driving in the night. As it passed he saw the sign of the hand of Fatima on one side. It shone in the dark. It was a good idea of yours, to put luminous② paint on a glove — it only

---

① evidence *n.* 证据 ② luminous *adj.* 发光的

shows up at night.'

'It works well,' said Jessop, 'but it's dangerous, because the people in the car can see it, too.'

'It cannot be seen in daylight, said Leblanc. 'And the hand of Fatima is a popular religious sign — it is painted on many different vehicles.'

'That's true,' agreed Jessop, 'but we must still be careful. If they did notice it, it could be a false trail.'

The next morning Leblanc excitedly brought in some new evidence — three pearls arranged in a triangle, stuck together with chewing gum.

'Three pearls in a triangle,' said Jessop. 'That's our sign to say that the next part of the journey was by plane.'

'You're right,' said Leblanc. 'This was found on an old army airfield, in a very lonely place. It is not used any more, but there were signs that a plane landed and left there not long ago.'

'Another plane,' said Jessop slowly. 'So now there is no trail and we don't know where they've gone. Again they have left for an unknown destination.'

Chapter 15

'I can't believe,' thought Hilary, 'that I've been here ten days!' The most frightening thing was how quickly and easily she had adapted to life in the Unit. After only a week she had begun to accept her way of life as natural. It was a strange life, where nothing was real — like living in a dream. Perhaps she would always feel like she was living in a dream... perhaps she would never wake up.

It was interesting, thought Hilary, to see how her fellow-travellers reacted to life in the Unit. She didn't meet Helga Needheim very often, but the German woman seemed happy and satisfied. Dr Barron, who Hilary sometimes talked to, was impressed with the working conditions and loved his work — although he admitted that he had not expected to live in a prison.

'But I was paid a large amount of money before I came here,' he added. 'And when all this comes to an end, I will be able to spend it.'

'When all this comes to an end?' Hilary repeated. 'Why should that happen?'

'My dear,' said Dr Barron, 'nothing is permanent. In time, the Unit will break up and fall apart. What happens here is too strange, too unreal. It will not last. But until that happens, I am happy to work here.'

Torquil Ericsson also seemed to be quite happy living in the Unit. Hilary didn't understand him. He seemed to live in a world of his own, a world that didn't really exist. Only he could see this ideal world where the scientists ruled and controlled everything — it existed only in his own head.

Andy Peters was easier for Hilary to understand. Like her, Peters hated living in the Unit.

'I had no idea what it would really be like,' he told Hilary. 'I have to get out of here.'

'It won't be easy,' said Hilary quietly. They were walking together on the roof garden.

'No,' said Peters, 'it won't be easy, but it's not impossible. Nothing's impossible.'

'I like to hear you say that,' said Hilary. 'I hate it here, but I'm more afraid that I'll get used to it.'

'Yes,' Peters said thoughtfully. 'I've wondered about that. What does your husband think? He's been here a while now.'

'Tom? I — oh, I don't know. It's so difficult. I —' Hilary was silent.

For ten days she had lived with — and shared a bedroom with — a man who was a complete stranger to her. She didn't understand Tom Betterton. He didn't seem to be upset by his real wife's death. All he could think about was getting away from the Unit. Again and again he said, 'I must get away from here. I must, I must.'

But the way he said this was very different to the way Peters said it. Peters was a young, angry man, confident that he would be able to escape. Tom Betterton sounded like a man who was about to collapse, a man who was almost crazy. Perhaps, Hilary thought suddenly, this was what she and Peters would be like in six months' time.

She wished she could talk to Andy Peters about this. She wished she could say, 'Tom Betterton isn't my husband. I know nothing about him and I don't know what to do or say to help him.' Instead she chose her words carefully. 'Tom seems like a stranger to me now. He doesn't — tell me things. Sometimes I think being shut up in here is driving him mad. How *can* we get out of here?'

'We've got to plan it very carefully, Olive,' Peters said. 'If there's a way in, there's a way out. We'll need to be clever and pretend to play a part — perhaps pay someone who works here to help — but we can do it. We will get out.'

'I'm sure *you* will,' said Hilary, 'but what about me?'

'Well, it's different for you.' Peters sounded embarrassed.

For a moment Hilary wondered what he meant, and then she realized that he was talking about Tom Betterton. She had come here to be with the man she loved — and she had got what she wanted.

Chapter 16

I

'Good evening, Mrs Betterton,' said Miss Jennson, her eyes shining with excitement behind her glasses. 'There will be a meeting tonight. The Director himself is going to speak to us. He's a wonderful man!'

'That's good,' said Andy Peters, as Miss Jennson moved away. 'I've been waiting to see this Director.'

'Tom said the Director is very inspiring,' said Hilary. 'But I don't really know what he meant.'

'I'm sure he can't be *that* wonderful,' said Peters with a smile.

'Oh, I'm so glad you're here,' said Hilary. 'You're so nice and ordinary. I'm sorry,' she said as Peters looked amused, 'that sounded rude.'

'So you like ordinary people?' Peters said. 'Not someone who's a genius?'

'Yes,' said Hilary. 'And you — you've changed since you came here. You don't seem so bitter① any more — you don't hate.'

But immediately his face looked grim②. 'That's not true,' he said. 'I can still hate. There are some things that *should* be hated.'

---

① bitter *adj.* 愤愤不平的　② grim *adj.* 严肃的

II

The meeting took place after dinner in the large lecture room. Hilary sat next to Tom Betterton. From the way Miss Jennson had spoken about him, Hilary was disappointed when the Director stepped up on the platform in front of them. He looked like a boring English businessman, heavy and middle-aged.

'First, I would like to welcome our new colleagues,' began the Director, before saying a few words about each of the new arrivals in French, German and English. After that he went on to speak of the aims and beliefs of the Unit.

Though she tried, afterwards Hilary couldn't really remember the Director's exact words — or perhaps the words themselves were just ordinary. But listening to the Director speak those words was a very different experience.

He spoke very simply, about Youth① and about Power — how the future would be shaped by the young scientists, and how together they would create a New World.

'Here in this Unit we are gathering the most intelligent young brains from all over the world,' the Director said. 'In time, we will have the scientific knowledge and power to destroy the world. When that day comes, we will be in charge of world affairs — we will control the whole world!'

It was not the words themselves, but the power of the speaker that affected the listening audience so intensely. When Hilary left the lecture room, in a state of high emotion, she could see that the other people around her felt the same — inspired and uplifted②. She felt almost drunk with the intense emotions that

---

① youth *n.* 年轻人   ② uplifted *adj.* 振奋的

the Director's words had produced.

Then she felt a hand on her arm. 'Come up to the roof garden,' said Andy Peters. 'We need some air.'

They went up in the lift without speaking and stepped out among the palm trees under the stars.

Peters breathed in deeply. 'Yes, that's better.' He shook Hilary's arm. 'Come on, Olive,' he said. 'You don't really believe all that. We've heard it all before.'

'But it would be wonderful,' said Hilary with enthusiasm. 'It would be a wonderful world!'

'Think about it properly,' said Peters sharply. 'Youth and brains — what does it really mean? Here that means Helga Needheim, ruthless and arrogant, and Torquil Ericsson, an impractical dreamer. Or Dr Barron, who would sell his grandmother to get money for his work. And your own husband, a man too frightened and nervous to work at all. And these people are going to rule the world? Don't make me laugh! It's all total nonsense!'

Hilary sat down. 'I do believe you're right,' she said at last. 'But it was a wonderful idea. How does the Director make everyone feel like that?'

'I don't know how he does it,' said Peters, 'but I'm glad you're back to normal now.' Then suddenly his manner changed. 'I suppose I shouldn't have brought you straight up here. What will your husband say?'

'He probably won't even notice,' said Hilary.

'I'm sorry, Olive. It must be hard for you to see him like this.'

'We must get out of here,' said Hilary passionately. 'We must!'

'We will,' Peters said. 'I've made some progress. There are

lots of people here who aren't happy. I'll get you out, Olive.'

'And Tom, too?'

Peters's face darkened. 'Listen, Olive, it's best if Tom stays here. He'll be — safer here than in the outside world.'

'Safer? I don't know what you mean,' said Hilary. 'Do you think he's going mad?'

'No,' said Peters slowly. 'But a cage can be a safe place.'

Suddenly Hilary remembered that Tom had said that the police were looking for him. But being in a real prison would still be better than staying here. 'Tom must come, too,' she insisted.

'All right, but I've warned you,' said Peters bitterly. 'I wish I knew why you care so much for that man.'

Hilary stared at him. She said nothing, but she wanted to say, 'I don't care for him. He means nothing to me.' She wanted to say, 'The man I care about is *you* ...'

III

'Have you been enjoying yourself with your American friend?' Tom Betterton said as Hilary entered their bedroom. He looked at her closely, as if seeing her for the first time. 'You're a good-looking woman, Olive,' he said. From the beginning Hilary had insisted that he should always call her by his wife's name. 'Once I would have noticed that. I'm a normal man — or I used to be.'

Hilary sat down beside him. 'What *is* the matter with you, Tom?'

'I've told you. I can't think,' he said. 'I can't work.'

'The others don't seem to feel the same as you,' said Hilary. 'It would help if you had a real friend here.'

'I've seen a lot of Torquil Ericsson lately,' said Tom. 'He's a brilliant man.'

'He's a strange man,' said Hilary. 'I think he's frightening.'

'Frightening? Torquil? He's actually very gentle — and like a child in some ways.'

'Tom,' said Hilary, 'don't get too friendly with Torquil Ericsson.'

'Why not?' He stared at her.

'I don't know,' Hilary said. 'It's just a feeling I have.'

Chapter 17

I

'They must have left Africa,' said Leblanc.

'I'm not so sure,' said Jessop. 'Only a small plane could have used that army airfield. It would need to refuel① before it crossed the sea.'

'But I tell you, my friend,' said Leblanc, 'we have searched everywhere. Even if your agent② has used the spray...'

'If my agent has used the spray,' said Jessop, 'we will know eventually. We just haven't found the right plane yet.' He paused. 'I wonder — perhaps instead of flying North, they flew back again — and flew South.'

'But where would they go?' asked Leblanc. 'There are only the High Atlas mountains — and after that, the desert...'

II

'You promise? You promise that I will be able to go to America?'

'Yes, I promise, Mohammed. If we get out of here, you'll be on your way. Tell me, why do you want to go to America?'

'This country is not modern — I do not wish to stay here all my life. The brother of my wife has gone to America, so I have family there.'

---

① refuel *v.* 补充燃料   ② agent *n.* 特工

Peters looked thoughtfully at the dignified, dark-skinned face. Mohammed in his white robes was an impressive sight. 'Of course, if we are found out...'

Mohammed smiled, showing his beautiful white teeth. 'Then it is death — for me certainly, though perhaps not for you.'

'Do you know what you have to do?' Peters asked.

'I must take you up to the roof garden after dark. Also, I must put some clothing in your room — such as I and the other servants wear. Later — there will be other things.'

'That's right. I had better go now — somebody may notice we're staying a long time in the lift.'

III

There was dancing that evening. Andy Peters was dancing with Miss Jennson. He held her close to him and whispered in her ear. He winked① at Hilary as he passed.

Hilary tried not to smile, and looked away. Then she frowned as she saw Tom Betterton talking to Torquil Ericsson.

'Olive, will you dance with me?' asked Simon Murchison.

'Yes, of course, Simon,' said Hilary, though she could see he was a bad dancer.

'I like your dress, Olive,' Murchison said as they danced. 'They really do give you everything you need here. I know it can take time to get used to it, but after a while...'

'You mean people can get used to anything?'

'Well, some people adjust② better than others,' said Murchison. 'Tom doesn't seem very happy, though. Is he here? Oh

---

① wink *v.* 眨眼 ② adjust *v.* 调整

yes, I see him — he's talking to Torquil. They're very friendly now.'

The dance ended and Hilary danced next with Andy Peters.

'I managed to get some information from Miss Jennson,' he told her. 'There's a group of important people visiting here tomorrow.'

'Andy — do you think there might be a chance...'

'No, I don't,' said Peters, 'but we'll get to know what happens — the routine. And then next time... I'll talk sweetly to Miss Jennson and see what else I can find out.'

'What do the visitors know about this place?'

'About us — the Unit, I mean — nothing at all. They're here to see the leper colony and the hospital. This place has been built into the mountain, so you can't see how big it really is. And our area is shut off from the main building.'

'Our life here — it's still so unreal.'

'I know,' agreed Peters. 'I can't get used to not seeing any children about. And now you're here, you must be glad that you don't have children — they certainly wouldn't like to be indoors all the time!'

He felt Hilary's body suddenly grow tense. 'I'm sorry — have I said the wrong thing?' He took her to sit down. 'I'm sorry,' he said again.

'It's not your fault,' said Hilary. 'I did have a child — and she died — that's all.'

'You had a child?' Peters stared, surprised. 'I thought you'd only been married to Betterton for six months?'

Hilary's face reddened. 'Yes, of course,' she said, 'but I was — married before.'

'Oh, I see. I didn't know that. It's strange to think that I don't really know anything about you.'

'And I don't know anything about you,' said Hilary, glad to change the subject. 'Tell me about your family.'

'I was brought up in a very scientific household,' said Peters. 'No one ever thought of anything but science. But I wasn't the clever one — that was the girl in the family. She was brilliant — a genius. She could have been as famous as Marie Curie.'

'She — what happened to her?'

'She was killed,' he said abruptly.

'She must have been killed in the war,' thought Hilary. 'You cared about her?' she asked gently.

'More than I have ever cared about anybody.'

Peters shook his head quickly. 'Let's not talk about that.' It was his turn to change the subject. 'Look at Ericsson,' he said. 'He's so formal — he looks as if he's made of wood.'

'It's because he's so tall and thin.'

'He's not that tall. He's actually about the same height as me — five foot eleven or six foot.'

'He looks taller,' said Hilary. 'Height can be deceptive①.'

'Yes,' agreed Peters. 'It's like descriptions on passports. Ericsson's passport probably says: Height six foot, fair hair, blue eyes, nose medium. From that description you still wouldn't know what Torquil really looked like. What's the matter?'

'Nothing.' Hilary was staring across the room at Ericsson. That was exactly how Jessop had described Boris Glydr! Was *that* why she had always felt nervous of Torquil Ericsson?

Turning abruptly to Peters she said, 'I suppose he *is* Ericsson? He couldn't be someone else?'

---

① deceptive *adj.* 有欺骗性的

Peters looked at her in astonishment. 'I don't think so. Ericsson is quite a well-known scientist. And who else could he be? It's not very likely.'

'No,' said Hilary. 'No, of course it isn't likely.'

Of course Ericsson was not Boris Glydr. But why had Olive Betterton wanted to warn Tom about Boris? Was it because she knew that Boris Glydr was on his way to the Unit? What if he was really Torquil Ericsson?

Just then the Deputy Director stepped forward to make an announcement.

'Friends and colleagues,' said Dr Van Heidem, 'tomorrow you are asked to remain in the Emergency Area for twenty-four hours. Please meet at eleven a.m. I am sorry for the inconvenience.'

'I must go and dance again with Miss Jennson,' said Peters as the music re-started. 'I'll see if I can find out any more information.' He moved away, leaving Hilary with her thoughts. Torquil Ericsson? Boris Glydr?

IV

At eleven the next morning, everyone met in the large lecture room, where a careful check was made to ensure they were all there. Then they went on a long walk through endless twisting white corridors. Hilary knew that Peters had a small compass[①] hidden in his hand, and was calculating where they were going. 'It doesn't help now,' he whispered, 'but it might help in the future.'

At the end of one corridor they all stopped in front of a door

---

① compass n. 指南针

while it was opened. Peters took out his cigarette case. 'No smoking, please,' said Van Heidem sharply. 'You have been told that already.'

'Sorry, Sir.' Peters paused with the cigarette case in his hand. Then they all went forward again — 'just like sheep,' thought Hilary.

'The women will sleep in the room on the right,' said Miss Jennson. 'The men will have the room on the left.'

The room where all the women were going to sleep looked rather like a hospital. It had beds all down each side of the room, separated by plastic curtains. There was also a bathroom, and the living room, which was shared with the men, was through a door at the end.

Two films were shown during the day in the shared living room to help pass the time. In the evening, Peters sat next to Miss Jennson, while Hilary played cards with Dr Barron, and Simon and Bianca Murchison. She enjoyed the game, and it was half past eleven when they finished.

'It's quite late now,' said Hilary. 'I suppose the visitors have gone home?' All day she had felt helpless, knowing that nearby there were people from the outside, but with no way of asking them for help.

'I don't really know,' said Simon Murchison. 'Sometimes they stay the night, but they will be gone by lunchtime tomorrow.'

'Is that when we go back to our apartments?' Hilary asked.

'Yes,' said Bianca Murchison. 'Everything here is so well arranged.'

She and Hilary got up and said good night. But just as Hilary was entering the women's bedroom, she felt a soft touch on her arm. She turned sharply to find one of the tall, dark-skinned servants.

'Madame, you are to come,' he said in French.

'Come? Come where?'

'Please follow me.'

She hesitated for a moment, then followed the man doubtfully through a door and along many white corridors. She had no idea where they were going. At the end of one corridor the man pressed a button on the wall and a small lift appeared. They got in.

'Where are you taking me?' Hilary asked.

'To the Master, Madame. It is a great honour.'

The lift stopped, and they walked down yet another corridor until they reached a door. When she walked through it, Hilary found herself inside a luxurious room, filled with comfortable sofas and beautiful rugs.

She stared in astonishment. Sitting on a sofa was a little old man with a yellow-tinted face — Mr Aristides.

Chapter 18

'Please sit down, dear Madame,' said Mr Aristides.

In a dream, Hilary sat down opposite the old man, who laughed at her surprise. 'So, you did not expect to see me here?' he said.

'No, indeed,' said Hilary. 'I never thought —' but already her surprise was beginning to fade. When she saw Mr Aristides, the dream world in which she had been living for the last few weeks fell apart and broke. The Unit had seemed so unreal, because it *was* unreal. It was all a show — it had never been what it pretended to be.

'I understand now,' said Hilary. 'This — is all yours, isn't it?'

'Yes, Madame.'

'And the Director?'

'He is very good,' said Mr Aristides. 'I pay him very well. He used to run religious meetings.'

He thoughtfully smoked his cigarette. 'As you know, Madame, I am one of the richest men in the world. I wanted to use my wealth to help humanity. The hospital I have built here is researching a cure for leprosy①. Even in these modern times people have a fear of leprosy, and will not come near a leper colony. It makes a very useful disguise.'

'So that's why this place is a leper colony,' said Hilary.

'Yes. We are also researching cancer and other diseases — well-known doctors and other important people often come

---

① leprosy *n*. 麻风

here to see and admire our work. But the secret part of the hospital cannot be seen, even from a plane. And of course, I would never be suspected.' He smiled. 'No one would suspect me of anything, because I am so very rich.'

'But why?' asked Hilary. 'I don't understand why.'

'I am a businessman,' said Mr Aristides simply. 'I am also a collector. In the past I have collected paintings, sculptures and Chinese pottery. Now I collect brains — I am slowly collecting all the intelligent young scientists in the world and bringing them here. One day every country will realize that all their scientists are old. All the young brains — the doctors, the chemists, the physicists, the surgeons — are all *here*. So, if they want a scientist, they will have to come and buy them from me!'

'You mean...' Hilary stared at him. 'You mean that all this is just for money?'

'Of course,' nodded Mr Aristides. 'Otherwise, it would not make sense, would it?'

Hilary sighed deeply. 'No,' she said slowly. 'It wouldn't make sense.' She paused. 'But how do you get all these people to come here?'

'I buy them, Madame, just as I buy anything else. I buy them with money or with ideas and beliefs. If they have broken the law, I buy them by offering safety.'

'That explains,' said Hilary thoughtfully, 'why everyone here is so different.'

'As I thought, Madame, you are intelligent. I had you brought to Fez so I could take a look at you. I was pleased that you were coming here,' continued Mr Aristides. 'These scientists, they are not interesting to talk to. Their wives, too, are often dull. Indeed, wives are only allowed here if their husbands can't work properly without them.' He paused. 'This seemed to be the case with your husband. Tom Betterton is a genius, but his work here has been very disappointing.'

'But doesn't that happen all the time?' asked Hilary. 'These people are in prison. How can they work properly if they aren't free?'

'They are like birds in a cage,' said Mr Aristides. 'Eventually they will forget they were ever free. Then they will all obey.'

'But if you sell scientists for money,' argued Hilary, 'surely once they go back to the real world they can refuse to work for their new employer? They'll be free again — free to do exactly what they want.'

'Yes, that is true,' said the old man. 'But we are working on different ways to make people behave. We have been experimenting[①] with a brain operation that will make people happy and content — but without any desire to be free.'

'You've been experimenting?' cried Hilary. 'On human beings?'

'We experiment on people who did not obey,' said Mr Aristides. 'Such people have their uses.'

Hilary stared at him. She felt a deep horror of this smiling, yellow-faced little man who talked so casually about human life. He seemed so reasonable and so businesslike, which only made the horror worse.

'You talk of freedom, Madame,' the old man continued, 'and I know you are talking about your husband. I am disappointed in Tom Betterton. And his work has not improved since you arrived.'

---

① experiment v. 试验

'So let him go,' said Hilary. 'He won't tell anyone about this place, I promise.'

'Perhaps,' said Mr Aristides thoughtfully, 'he would not talk if you stayed behind, as a hostage①. Would you do that, Madame?'

Hilary stared past him into the shadows. Would she stay here so that Tom Betterton could go free? But Mr Aristides didn't know that she wasn't Betterton's wife, that the woman he really loved was dead.

She lifted her head. 'Yes, I would stay here,' she said.

'You are brave, Madame, and loyal② and loving,' said the old man. 'These are good qualities. We will talk about this another time.'

'Oh no, no!' said Hilary suddenly, hiding her face in her hands. 'I can't bear it here!'

'You must not mind so much, Madame.' The old man's voice was soothing. 'You are horrified by my plans, but when you have thought about them, you will gradually come to accept them.'

'Never!' cried Hilary. 'Never!'

'Ah,' said Mr Aristides, 'you speak with the passion that women with red hair so often have. You have beautiful red hair — as did my second wife. I have enjoyed talking to you. When I visit here next time, we will talk again.'

'Please let me leave this place,' said Hilary desperately. 'Please!'

Mr Aristides shook his head. 'I can't do that,' he said gently. 'You would tell everyone about my plans.'

'I won't,' said Hilary. 'I promise I won't say a word. But I

---

① hostage *n.* 人质 ② loyal *adj.* 忠诚的

must get out of this prison!'

'I don't believe that you would keep my secret,' said Mr Aristides. 'And you came here willingly, to be with your husband. Here you have everything you need to live a pleasant life.'

He got up and touched Hilary gently on the shoulder. 'In a year or two, the red-haired bird will be happy in her cage,' he said. 'Though perhaps not as interesting...'

Chapter 19

I

Hilary awoke suddenly the next night and sat up, listening.

'Tom, do you hear that?'

'Yes. It's a plane, flying low. It happens now and then.'

'I wondered ...' She did not finish her sentence.

Hilary lay awake, thinking about her strange interview with Mr Aristides. She had not told Tom about it. The old man liked her. Could she somehow use that to escape?

II

'A message, at last,' said Leblanc with excitement. 'One of our pilots has been flying over the High Atlas mountains, and he saw a signal being flashed in Morse code①.'

He showed Jessop the message.

C-O-G-L-E-P-R-O-S-I-E-S-L

'We can ignore the COG and SL,' he said, crossing these letters out. 'They're our codes. This is the real message.'

LEPROSIE

Leblanc looked at it doubtfully. 'What can that mean?'

'Leprosy?' said Jessop. 'Are there any leper colonies in that

---

① Morse code n. 莫尔斯电码

area?'

Leblanc looked at a large map on the wall. 'Here,' he pointed, 'is where the pilot was flying. Let me think.' He paused for a few moments. 'Yes, I believe there is an important medical research hospital somewhere in this area. They are researching and treating leprosy there. But surely that can't be the place we want? It has an excellent reputation — the President of Morocco himself supports it.'

'A clever idea, then,' said Jessop. 'No one will expect that a respectable hospital is hiding the world's leading scientists. And only doctors are interested in a leper colony — no one else will want to visit it. Who owns and pays for the hospital?'

Leblanc left the room and came back a few minutes later with an official-looking book in his hand. 'The money comes from a group of wealthy people,' he said, 'but most of the money is supplied by charities① run by Mr Aristides.'

'So, the hospital is paid for by Mr Aristides,' said Jessop thoughtfully. 'And he was in Fez at the same time as Olive Betterton.'

'But, my friend, this is unbelievable!' exclaimed Leblanc. 'Aristides is so rich, so powerful! He is involved in everything — banks, factories, weapons, transport — everything! He sits in his castle in Spain and controls governments!'

'Then it isn't really so surprising that Aristides is involved,' said Jessop calmly. 'As you say, Leblanc, he is a man of enormous power and influence. We were stupid not to think of him before. The question is,' he added, 'what are we going to do about it?'

'It won't be easy,' said Leblanc, calming down. 'And if we

---

① charity *n*. 慈善组织

are wrong — I don't dare think of it! Even if we are right, we still have to *prove* that we are right. And if we investigate, we could be told to stop — by some powerful and important people. No, my friend, it won't be easy...' He paused. 'But we will do it.'

Chapter 20

Several expensive cars arrived in front of the hospital's huge iron gates. Inside were a French Minister①, the American ambassador, a retired top British judge② and a journalist who worked for a very famous newspaper. Leblanc and Jessop were also inside one of the cars.

'I hope,' said the French Minister nervously, 'that we don't actually *meet* the lepers.'

'No, no,' said the ambassador. 'I'm told we'll be quite safe. And I believe the medical treatment of lepers here is very advanced.'

The huge gates opened, and the visitors were greeted by the Deputy Director, Dr Van Heidem. 'Welcome, welcome, my friends,' he said. 'As promised, Mr Aristides himself has arrived from Spain, and he is waiting for you inside. Please follow me.'

Mr Aristides greeted his visitors in a large comfortable lounge, where they were served drinks by the dark-skinned servants dressed in white robes.

'This is a wonderful place,' said the French Minister, looking round.

'Yes, I am very proud of my hospital,' said Mr Aristides. 'It is my final gift to humanity. No expense has been spared.'

'And we're doing very important work here,' added Van Heidem with enthusiasm. 'We are getting very good results in our treatment of leprosy and other diseases.'

---

① minister *n*. 公使 ② judge *n*. 法官

A delicious meal was served to the visitors, who were hungry after their long journey to the hospital. They were given fine wines to drink and were feeling very contented when they began their tour of the hospital.

The tour took two hours, and was very thorough. The visitors were impressed with the expensive medical equipment, the well-qualified staff and the endless white corridors. Some people asked detailed questions about living conditions and the people who worked there, which Van Heidem answered easily. Jessop and Leblanc walked behind the others.

'We haven't found anything yet,' whispered Leblanc, his voice worried. 'It has taken me weeks to arrange this visit. If we are wrong about this, we will lose our jobs!'

'It's not over yet,' said Jessop. 'Our friends are here, I'm sure of it. It's not really surprising that they are hard to find.'

'But we need evidence!' said Leblanc. 'If there is no evidence, nothing will be done. The French Minister, the American ambassador — they don't believe us. They say that Aristides is above suspicion.'

'Keep calm, Leblanc,' replied his colleague. 'I do have some evidence that our friends are here. I'm carrying a very small machine that has detected signs of radioactivity[①]— just as we planned. All these corridors are meant to confuse us, but there is part of the building that we have not seen.'

'But you know it is there because you have detected signs of radioactivity?'

'Exactly,' said Jessop. 'It is just the same as when we found the pearls and the paint on the door of the car. This time we can't actually *see* anything, but the signs are there.'

---

① radioactivity *n.* 放射性

'But is that enough, my friend?' asked Leblanc. 'Is that enough evidence to convince people who do not want to believe?'

'Perhaps this evidence won't convince all of them,' said Jessop, 'but I hope it will convince some of them. There's the journalist — he would love to have such a big story for his newspaper. And there's the man who used to be the top judge in Britain. He may be old, but he is still a man of great intelligence — and he won't ignore evidence.'

When the tour was over the visitors were served more drinks in the lounge. The French Minister congratulated Mr Aristides on establishing such a fine hospital. 'And now,' he said, 'it is time for us to leave. We have seen *everything*,' — he paused — 'and we are very impressed with the work you are doing here.'

Into the silence a voice suddenly spoke. 'I would like to ask a question, if I may,' said Jessop.

'Of course,' said Dr Van Heidem. 'What would you like to know?'

'We've met a lot of people who work here,' said Jessop, 'but there's one person — a friend of mine — who I haven't seen.'

'A friend of yours?' Dr Van Heidem said politely, surprised.

'Well, two friends actually,' said Jessop, 'Tom and Olive Betterton. I believe they're both here. Can I talk to them before I go?'

Dr Van Heidem's reactions were perfect. His eyes opened in wide and polite surprise. He frowned in a puzzled way. 'Betterton — Betterton — no, I'm afraid we have no one of that name here.'

'There's an American, too,' said Jessop. 'Andrew Peters, a

nuclear chemist, I believe.' He turned to the American ambassador. 'Am I right, Sir?'

The ambassador looked at Jessop and took a long time to answer. 'Yes, you're right,' he said at last. 'I would like to see Andrew Peters.'

Van Heidem still looked confused. Jessop looked quickly at Mr Aristides. The old man's face showed nothing.

'You know the name of Thomas Betterton, don't you?' Jessop asked Van Heidem.

Just for a second Van Heidem hesitated. He started to turn his head towards Mr Aristides, but stopped himself in time. 'Thomas Betterton,' he said. 'Why, yes, I think...'

'He disappeared six months ago,' said the journalist. 'It was front-page news all over the world. The police have been looking for Betterton everywhere. And you say he's here?'

'No!' said Van Heidem sharply. 'You are mistaken. Betterton is not here. You have seen everything there is to see.'

'Not everything,' said Jessop quietly. 'We haven't seen a young man called Torquil Ericsson, or Dr Barron.'

'Ah!' said Van Heidem. 'I understand now. You are talking about the people who were killed here in Morocco — in a plane crash. It was very sad.'

'So, I am wrong?' said Jessop. 'You say these people are not here?'

'But how can they be, my dear Sir, since they were all killed in this plane crash? All their bodies were found, I believe.'

'The bodies,' said Jessop slowly and clearly, 'were too burned to be identified.'

There was a movement behind him. 'So the bodies of these people could not be properly identified?' asked the retired

British judge, Lord Alverstoke.

'No, my lord,' said Jessop, 'and I have evidence that at least one person — Mrs Betterton — survived the plane crash.'

'Evidence? What evidence, Mr Jessop?' said Lord Alverstoke.

'Mrs Betterton was wearing a necklace of pearls when she left Fez,' explained Jessop. 'One of these pearls was found half a mile from where the plane crashed.'

'How do you know that this pearl came from Mrs Betterton's necklace?'

'Because my colleague, Monsieur Leblanc, and I marked all the pearls,' said Jessop. 'We believed that Mrs Betterton was going to join her husband, Tom Betterton, who is wanted by the police. More pearls were found, and we also found a mark on a car, carrying six people, which was made by one of the passengers with luminous paint.'

'Very interesting,' said Lord Alverstoke. 'Very interesting indeed.'

'And where was this car last seen?' asked Mr Aristides, coming to life.

'At an old army airfield, Sir.' Jessop told them the exact location.

'That is hundreds of miles from here,' said Mr Aristides. 'Even if you are right, and the plane crash was faked, why do you think these people are *here*?'

'One of our pilots saw a signal,' said Jessop, 'saying that these people were at a leper colony.'

'It is an interesting idea,' said Mr Aristides. 'But you are wrong, quite wrong. These people are not here.' He spoke with calm authority. 'But you are welcome to search for them.'

'I'd like to do that,' said Jessop. 'We'll start our search in the fourth corridor from the second laboratory, turning to the left at the end.'

Dr Van Heidem made a sudden surprised movement, and a glass crashed to the floor. Jessop smiled.

'It is an interesting idea,' Mr Aristides said again, gently. He looked at his watch. 'But you will excuse me, gentlemen, if I suggest that you should leave now. You have a long drive back to the airport.'

Both Leblanc and Jessop realized that this was an important moment. Mr Aristides was using his strong personality, daring them to accuse[①] him openly. The Minister just wanted to leave without doing anything, and though the others weren't sure, they hesitated to act against someone so rich and powerful as Mr Aristides. And Jessop and Leblanc couldn't act without the support of someone in authority, someone important.

'I do not think,' said a cold, clear voice into the silence, 'that we should leave just yet.' It was Lord Alverstoke. 'There appear to be questions that need to be answered.'

'But this is ridiculous,' said Mr Aristides. 'There is no evidence, no proof at all that these people are here.'

'Yes, there is.' Dr Van Heidem turned round in surprise, and everyone stared at the Moroccan servant who had stepped forward. He was a tall man with a dark face and was wearing white robes — but he had spoken with a strong American accent.

'Andrew Peters, Torquil Ericsson, Tom and Olive Betterton and Dr Barron are all here.' The man took a step towards the American ambassador. 'I know it's rather hard to recognize me at the moment, Sir,' he said, 'but I am Andrew Peters.'

---

① accuse *v*. 指责

Mr Aristides made a faint, angry noise before sitting back in his chair. There was no expression on his face.

'There are many scientists hidden away here,' said Peters. 'There's a whole secret area that you haven't seen.'

'Goodness me!' exclaimed the American ambassador. He looked closely at the man in front of him. 'Even now, Peters, I can hardly recognize you with that dark colouring on your face. What's your official FBI① number?'

'81347128, Sir.'

'And your initials?' asked the Ambassador.

'B.A.P.G., Sir.' The ambassador nodded. 'That is correct,' he said. 'And you say, Peters, that there are many scientists living here?'

'Yes, Sir. Some are here willingly, and some are not.'

'In that case,' said the Minister, stepping forward, 'there must be a thorough investigation.'

'Just a moment, please.' Mr Aristides raised a hand. 'It would seem that I have been very wrong to trust the people in charge here.' He looked coldly at Dr Van Heidem. 'I do not know exactly what you have been doing here, Van Heidem, but I obviously know nothing about it — nothing at all.'

There was authority in Mr Aristides' voice. 'If you have been keeping scientists here,' he continued, 'it is now over. And I'm sure I do not need to tell you, gentlemen,' — he turned to the visitors — 'that if anything has happened here that is against the law, it is nothing to do with me.'

'Because of the wealth, power and influence of the famous Mr Aristides, he would not be arrested,' thought Jessop. But he had been defeated②, and his plan had failed.

---

① FBI *n*. 联邦调查局 ② defeat *v*. 打败

The Minister turned to Van Heidem. 'I repeat,' he said, 'that there must be a thorough investigation.'

Van Heidem's face was pale. 'Come this way,' he said. 'I will show you everything.'

Chapter 21

'I feel like I've woken up from a nightmare,' sighed Hilary, stretching her arms above her head. They had arrived that morning at a hotel in Tangier, and were now sitting outside on the terrace.

'Yes, it was a nightmare,' agreed Tom Betterton, 'but it's over now.'

Jessop came along the terrace and sat down beside them. 'Where's Andy Peters?' asked Hilary.

'He'll be here soon,' said Jessop. 'He has something to do first.'

'So Peters was one of your agents,' said Hilary. 'He put luminous paint on that car and used his lead cigarette case to leave behind signs of radioactivity. I had no idea what he was doing.'

'No,' said Jessop, 'you were both very good at keeping secrets. And Peters isn't really one of my agents — he works for America.'

'So that's what you meant when you said I would have protection if I reached Tom. You meant Andy Peters.'

Jessop nodded. 'And I hope you're not disappointed,' he said, 'that in the end you didn't die.'

Hilary shook her head in disbelief. 'Now I can't believe that I ever wanted to end my life,' she said. 'I've been Olive Betterton so long that it's confusing to be Hilary Craven again.'

'Ah,' said Jessop, standing up. 'There's my friend, Leblanc. I must go and speak to him.' He walked along the terrace, leaving Tom and Hilary alone.

'Will you do one more thing for me?' asked Betterton

quickly.

'Yes, of course. What is it?' Hilary asked.

'Walk along the terrace with me, and then say that I've gone up to my room.'

'Why? What are you ...?'

'I'm leaving now,' he said, 'while I still can. If I stay here, I'll be arrested.'

Hilary looked at him with surprise — she had forgotten Betterton's problems. 'But where will you go?'

'Anywhere,' he said. 'I've got money hidden away under a different name.'

'So you *did* take money?'

'Of course I took money.'

'But they'll find you eventually.'

'I don't think so. Don't you realize that my face is different after the plastic surgery? They have an old description of me. I'll be safe.'

Hilary looked at him doubtfully. 'Isn't it better to be arrested?' she said. 'You won't stay in prison for long. But if you go now, you'll be hunted for the rest of your life.'

'You don't understand,' he said. 'You don't understand at all. Come on, let's go.'

Hilary walked with him slowly along the terrace. She didn't know what to do or what to say. Despite everything they'd shared, Tom Betterton was still a stranger to her.

They arrived at a door to the road. 'I'll go out here,' said Betterton. 'Goodbye.'

'Good luck,' said Hilary slowly.

But as Betterton opened the door, two men stood there,

blocking① his way. 'Thomas Betterton, you are under arrest,' said the first man, a police official. The second man moved behind Betterton to block his escape.

Betterton laughed. 'There's only one problem,' he said. 'I'm not Thomas Betterton. I've been calling myself Thomas Betterton but I'm not really him. I met Betterton in Paris and took his place. Ask this lady if you don't believe me.' He pointed to Hilary. 'She pretended to be my wife.' Hilary nodded.

'But because I'm *not* Tom Betterton,' he continued, 'I didn't know what his wife looked like. I thought she *was* Olive Betterton.'

'So *that's* why you pretended to know me!' exclaimed Hilary.

Betterton laughed again. 'I'm not Tom Betterton,' he repeated. 'Look at any photo of him and you'll see I'm telling the truth.'

The second man stepped forward. It was Andy Peters, and when he spoke his voice was cold and hard. 'I know you don't look like your photo any more,' he said. 'But you *are* Tom Betterton — and I can prove it.'

He held Betterton's arm firmly and took off the man's jacket. 'If you *are* Tom Betterton, you have a scar② in the shape of a Z in the bend③ of your right elbow④.' As he spoke, he ripped⑤ the shirtsleeve upwards.

'There it is,' Peters said, pointing. 'There are two laboratory assistants in America who will swear⑥ that that scar belongs to Tom Betterton. I know about it because Elsa wrote and told

---

① block *v.* 阻拦　② scar *n.* 伤疤　③ bend *n.* 弯曲　④ elbow *n.* 肘部
⑤ rip *v.* 撕　⑥ swear *v.* 发誓

me.'

'*Elsa?*' Betterton stared at him. He began to shake nervously. 'Elsa? What about Elsa?'

'She is the reason you are being arrested,' replied Peters.

'You are under arrest for murder,' the police official said. 'The murder of your first wife, Elsa Betterton.'

Chapter 22

'I'm so sorry, Olive,' said Andy Peters. 'You must believe that. Because of you, I would have given Betterton another chance. I warned you that he would be safer if he stayed in the Unit — even though I've come halfway across the world to make him pay for what he did to Elsa.'

'I don't understand,' said Hilary. 'Who are you?'

'I thought you knew,' said Peters. 'My real name is Boris Andrei Pavlov Glydr — I'm Elsa's cousin, from Poland. I went to university in America and became an American citizen called Andrew Peters. When the war began, I went back to Europe and helped Elsa and my uncle escape from Germany. Elsa — I've told you about Elsa. She was a brilliant scientist. It was Elsa who really discovered ZE Fission. Tom Betterton was working as an assistant to my uncle, Dr Mannheim, and he married Elsa on purpose because he realized how important her work was. When Elsa discovered ZE Fission, he poisoned her.'

'Oh, no, no.'

'No one suspected him then,' said Peters. 'Betterton pretended to be heartbroken by Elsa's death, and worked very hard. Then he announced that he had discovered ZE Fission. He got what he wanted — fame① and importance. Then he came to England and worked at Harwell.

'I was uneasy about the last letter I had received from Elsa. Her illness and later her death seemed very mysterious. When I finally got back to America I started asking questions, and I had

---

① fame n. 名望

medical tests done on her body, which proved that Elsa was poisoned. One of Betterton's friends, Walter Griffiths, heard about this, and must have told Betterton when he visited him in England. Betterton became nervous, and when he was approached by Aristides' agent — a woman called Carol Speeder — he decided to disappear, rather than be arrested for murder. He asked for plastic surgery to change his face. He was never a brilliant scientist — that's why he couldn't work properly at the Unit.'

'So you followed him?' asked Hilary.

'Yes. I was so determined to find Betterton that I followed him to the Unit. One of my scientist friends had also been approached by Carol Speeder. When I came to England I pretended that I was disappointed with my life, and that I wanted to share my scientific knowledge — and soon she approached me, too.' His face looked grim. 'Elsa was an important scientist and a beautiful and gentle woman. She was killed by the man she loved and trusted, who then took credit for① her brilliant work.'

'I see now,' said Hilary, 'I understand.'

'I wrote to you when I got to England,' said Peters, 'using my Polish name. I told you the facts.' He looked at her. 'I suppose you didn't believe me. You never answered. Then I went to the British Secret Service. I didn't trust anyone, but eventually Jessop and I made a plan together.' He paused. 'And now it's over. Betterton will be taken back to America where he will go on trial② for Elsa's murder.'

He stared down over the sunlit gardens towards the sea.

'And in the Unit,' he said slowly, 'I met you, Olive, and

---

① take credit for 因……受到好评 ② trial n. 审判

fell in love with you. But I'm the man responsible for sending your husband to prison — and perhaps death. I know you'll never forgive me for that. But I wanted to tell you everything myself before I go.' He stood up.

'Wait!' said Hilary, stretching out her hand. 'Wait. There's something you don't know. I'm not Betterton's wife. Olive Betterton died in the plane crash, and Jessop asked me to take her place.'

Peters stared at her in astonishment. 'You're *not* Olive Betterton?'

'No.'

'I don't believe it!' he said, sitting down heavily. 'Olive, my darling.'

'Don't call me Olive. My name's Hilary. Hilary Craven.'

'Hilary? I'll have to get used to that.' He put his hand over hers.

At the other end of the terrace, Jessop and Leblanc were talking. 'I'm afraid,' said the Frenchman, 'that we will not be able to arrest Aristides.'

'No,' said Jessop, looking over Leblanc's shoulder. 'He's too rich and powerful. But he's lost a lot of money, and he's old — he can't live forever.'

'What are you looking at, my friend?'

'Those two,' said Jessop. 'I sent Hilary Craven on a journey to an unknown destination. But it seems that her journey's end is the usual one after all. As Shakespeare says, "Journeys end in lovers meeting."'

文 化 注 释

World War II (1939 to 1945)
The war which Jessop refers to at the beginning of the book is the Second World War. The war began with the invasion of Poland by Nazi Germany on September 1, 1939. Great Britain, which had treaties with Poland, declared war on Germany when it refused to withdraw from Poland.

第二次世界大战(1939—1945)
本书开篇 Jessop 所指的战争为第二次世界大战。战争始于1939年9月1日,纳粹德国入侵波兰。英国当时与波兰签订有协议,于是当德国拒绝从波兰撤军时,英国对其宣战。

Nuclear fission
Nuclear fission is a nuclear reaction in which the nucleus of an atom is split into smaller parts, producing a massive amount of energy compared to that in a similar mass of chemical fuel such as gasoline. At the time of the story it was seen as a big advance, as it is a sustainable energy source. We now know that the products of this reaction are very radioactive and remain so for a significant amount of time. This gives rise to concerns over nuclear waste, as well as the potential to create nuclear weapons which can have devastating effects.

核裂变
核裂变是核反应的一种,借由将原子核分解为更小的部分产生大量的能量,相当于巨量汽油等化学燃料所产生的能量。在本书故事发生的时间,这被视为重要的进步,因为是一种可持续的能源。现在我们得知,这种反应的产物极具放射性,并会在很长一段时间内维持这种状态。这引起人们对于核废料的担忧,以及对于制造毁灭性核武器的可能的恐惧。

Harwell

This was the main centre for atomic energy research and development in the United Kingdom from the 1940s to the 1990s. Oxfordshire was chosen as a site for this because it was remote, had a good water supply and had good transport links. It was also close to a university with a nuclear physics laboratory. The laboratory was located on an airfield so that the aircraft hangars could contain the nuclear reactors. The laboratory was used to continue the research in nuclear fission both for military purposes and for generating energy.

哈韦尔中心

英国20世纪40年代至90年代的原子能研究和发展中心。选址在牛津郡的原因是此地较为偏僻,并且拥有优质的水源和便利的运输条件。此地还靠近一所拥有核物理实验室的大学。实验室建于机场内部,可以用机库来安放核反应堆。实验室主要用来继续进行核裂变方面的研究,同时满足军事以及生产能源的需要。

Morocco under French rule

Morocco remained independent until 1912. However, in the late 19th and early 20th centuries, the country became weak and unstable. This resulted in intervention by Europe to protect the

European investments which were threatened by the unrest. Europe also demanded economic privileges within the country. France established a protectorate over Morocco, which means that the country was protected by France against other countries. Although Morocco retained its autonomy as a 'state' under international law, it was controlled by the French government until 1956.

在法国统治下的摩洛哥
摩洛哥在1912年前为独立国家。但在19世纪末和20世纪初,该国国力衰退,局势动荡。结果导致欧洲介入,声称要保护受到动乱威胁的欧洲投资项目。欧洲还要求在该国内享有经济特权。法国后将该国接纳为保护国,意味着在面临他国威胁时将由法国对其进行保护。虽然摩洛哥按照国际法依然保留着"国家"的自治权,但直至1956年前均由法国政府控制。

Leprosy

Leprosy is a disease caused by bacteria (present in the nose and throat) which can cause damage to the skin, nerves, limbs and eyes. A person who has leprosy is called a leper. The disease was feared because it causes visible disfigurement and disability, and it was incurable and believed to be highly contagious. Therefore in the past, leper colonies were formed to create a place where people who had the disease could live together but isolated from the rest of society. These were quite widespread. Some colonies were located in remote locations to ensure quarantine. They were often run by monks or nuns.

Leprosy still exists today, but we now know that it is not transmitted as easily as people used to think. Leprosy colonies still exist in some regions around the world.

麻风

麻风是一种由细菌(见于鼻部和喉部)引起的疾病,可以对皮肤、神经、四肢和眼部造成伤害。患麻风的人称为 leper。人们对此病非常恐惧,因为其可以造成毁容和残疾,而且无法治愈,传染性极强。因此过去设有麻风病人隔离区,患病者聚集其中生活起居,与社会其他人士隔绝。此种隔离区分布很广。有些隔离区设在偏远地区,以保证隔离效果。通常由修士或者修女进行管理。

麻风今天依然存在,但我们现在得知,该病的传染性不像过去人们想象的那么强。麻风病人隔离区在世界某些地区依然存在。

Hand of Fatima

This is a sign depicting the open right hand. It represents blessings, power and strength and is believed to protect against evil. The name celebrates the daughter of the prophet Muhammed in the Islamic religion, although it also exists in other cultures with a different name, such as the hand of Mary in Christianity and the hand of Miriam in Jewish tradition.

法蒂玛之手

一种张开的右手造型的图案,代表祝福、权力和力量,人们相信其能抵御邪恶。名称来自伊斯兰教先知穆罕默德的女儿;该图案也见于其他文化,只是名称有所变化,例如基督教的玛丽之手(hand of Mary),以及犹太传统中的米利亚姆之手(hand of Miriam)。

Marie Curie: radioactivity

Marie Curie was a physicist and chemist, famous for her research on radioactivity. She was the first woman to receive a Nobel Prize for her work. Marie Curie received the Nobel Prize for Physics in 1903 and then went on to receive another Nobel Prize for Chemistry in 1911. She is one of only two people who have been awarded a Nobel Prize in two different fields. Sadly, because of her work on radioactive materials, she developed cancer and died in 1934.

居里夫人：放射性

物理学家、化学家居里夫人因其对于放射性的研究而闻名于世。她是第一位凭借自己的研究而获得诺贝尔奖的女性。1903年居里夫人获得当年的诺贝尔物理奖，然后又于1911年获得诺贝尔化学奖。只有两个人曾经在两个不同的领域获诺贝尔奖，居里夫人便是其中一位。不幸的是，由于工作中接触放射性原料，后来她患上了癌症，于1934年去世。

The Cold War

This story was written in 1954, some years after the beginning of the Cold War, which was a time of great tension between the USSR and USA. The Cold War (1946 – 1991) was the continuing state of political conflict, military tension and economic competition between the USSR and its allies, and the USA and its allies. The military forces never had a major battle but they competed to develop nuclear weapons, and in the race to put the first people into space. They also provided extensive aid to vulnerable states in order to gain support. Because the way of life in the USSR and the USA was so different, they saw each other as enemies and used spies to discover important information about each other. This led to a lot of suspicion between the two countries. The Cold War had times of relative calm, and times of high tension. It ended in 1991 when the USSR collapsed, leaving the USA as the dominant military power.

冷战

本书于 1954 年完成,当时冷战已经开始了几个年头,苏联和美国之间的关系异常紧张。冷战(1946—1991)指的是,苏联及其盟国与美国及其盟国之间政治冲突、军事紧张和经济竞争的持续状态。两方的军队从未大规模交火,但双方竞相发展核武器和载人航天活动。双方还向实力较弱的国家提供大规模援助,以此来获得支持。由于苏联和美国的生活方式大相径庭,双方都视彼此为敌人,并使用间谍来获取重要情报。这导致两方之间的怀疑与日俱增。冷战有相对平稳的时期,也有高度紧张的时期。1991 年苏联解体,冷战宣告结束,美国成为世界上最具统治力的军事大国。

Polish Resistance

The Polish Resistance movement in World War II was the largest resistance movement in the part of Europe which was occupied by the Nazis. It covered both the German and Soviet zones of occupation. It was an important part of the anti-fascist movement in Europe, and played an important part in disrupting German supply lines to the Eastern front. It also provided military intelligence to Britain, and was responsible for saving the lives of many Jewish people affected by the Holocaust.

波兰秘密抵抗组织
第二次世界大战中的波兰抵抗运动是欧洲纳粹占领区最大规模的抵抗运动。同时涉及德国和苏联的占领区。该运动是欧洲反法西斯运动的重要组成部分,在扰乱德国对东部战线的补给线方面发挥了重要作用。该运动还为英国提供了军事情报,并挽救了许多受到大屠杀威胁的犹太人的生命。

Creating a 'better world'
Because of the Cold War and the tension between the large countries of the world at this time, scientific work in this period was closely checked by governments — both from the scientist's own country, and also by spies from other countries. This is why the scientists, particularly Dr Barron, want to work somewhere away from society, where their work can be independent and secret.

创造一个"更美好的世界"
由于冷战和当时大国间的紧张关系,这一阶段的科学工作遭到政府的严密监控——既有来自科学家们自己国家对其的监控,也有国际上其他国家的间谍们对他们的监视。这就是那些科学家,尤其是 Dr Barron,希望在远离社会的地点工作的原因,这样他们的工作才能保持独立和私密。

Fellow-travellers
It is possible that Agatha Christie had a negative meaning attached to this phrase. In the 1950s it was used as a term to refer to a person who sympathized with the beliefs of an organization, or cooperated in its activities, but without having formal

membership in that group. In the early days of the Soviet Union, it was used without a negative meaning to describe writers and artists who shared the aims of the Russian Revolution but who didn't join the Communist party. When the phrase became fashionable in America in the 1940s and 1950s, it had taken on a negative meaning — for a person who held Communist beliefs even if they weren't fully part of the Communist party.

同路人

阿加莎·克里斯蒂可能使用了这个词的负面含义。20世纪50年代,本词用来形容那些同情某个组织的宗旨或者参与其活动,但并非组织正式成员的人。在苏联刚刚建立的时期,本词并没有负面含义,只是用来形容那些与俄国革命理念一致,但没有加入共产党的作家和艺术家。本词后来于20世纪40年代和50年代在美国流行起来,并被赋予了负面含义——描述那些虽然不是共产党员,但怀揣共产主义理想的人。

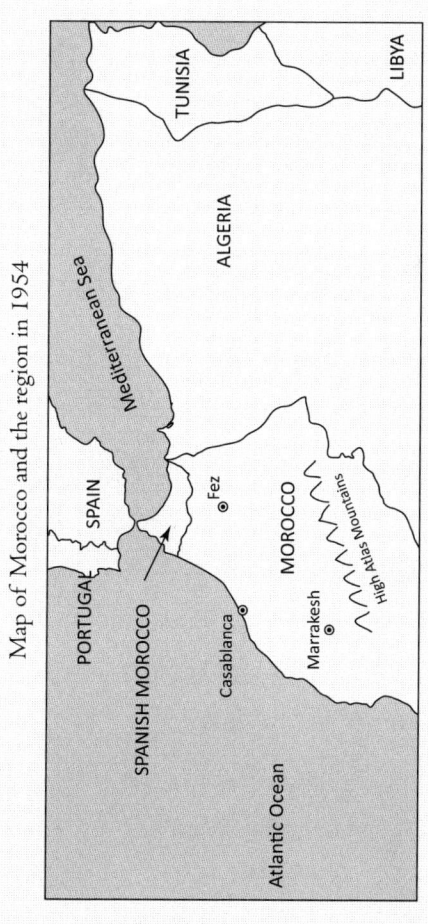

Map of Morocco and the region in 1954

阿加莎·克里斯蒂经典侦探作品集

怪屋(Crooked House)

密码(N or M?)

魔手(The Moving Finger)

<u>地狱之旅(Destination Unknown)</u>

古屋疑云(Peril at End House)

黑麦奇案(A Pocket Full of Rye)

借镜杀人(They Do It with Mirrors)

罗杰疑案(The Murder of Roger Ackroyd)

弄假成真(Dead Man's Folly)

书房命案(The Body in the Library)

死亡约会(Appointment with Death)

寓所谜案(The Murder at the Vicarage)

云中奇案(Death in the Clouds)

葬礼之后(After the Funeral)

鸽群中的猫(Cat Among the Pigeons)

命案目睹记(4.50 from Paddington)

闪光的氰化物(Sparkling Cyanide)

悬崖上的谋杀(Why Didn't They Ask Evans?)

穿棕色套装的人(The Man in the Brown Suit)

东方快车谋杀案(Murder on the Orient Express)

国际学舍谋杀案(Hickory Dickory Dock)

尼罗河上的惨案(Death on the Nile)

斯泰尔斯庄园奇案(The Mysterious Affair at Styles)

控方证人及其他(The Witness for the Prosecution and Other Stories)

图书在版编目(CIP)数据

地狱之旅:英文/(英)阿加莎·克里斯蒂著.—北京:商务印书馆,2019
(阿加莎·克里斯蒂经典侦探作品集)
ISBN 978-7-100-17408-4

Ⅰ.①地… Ⅱ.①阿… Ⅲ.①英语—语言读物②侦探小说—英国—现代 Ⅳ.①H319.4:I

中国版本图书馆CIP数据核字(2019)第082044号

权利保留,侵权必究。

阿加莎·克里斯蒂经典侦探作品集
地狱之旅
〔英〕阿加莎·克里斯蒂 著

商 务 印 书 馆 出 版
(北京王府井大街36号 邮政编码100710)
商 务 印 书 馆 发 行
北京市十月印刷有限公司印刷
ISBN 978-7-100-17408-4

2019年11月第1版　　开本 850×1168 1/32
2019年11月北京第1次印刷　印张 4⅜
定价:23.80元